RETIREMENT PLANNING

The Real Mid-Life Crisis

A Practical Guide to Secure Your Financial Future

DUANE D. FREESE

RETIREMENT PLANNING

The Real Mid-Life Crisis

A Practical
Guide to Secure
Your Financial
Future

DUANE D. FREESE

International Publishing Corporation
Chicago

Library of Congress Catalog Card Number: 90-084313

ISBN 0-942641-25-6

This publication is designed to provide accurate and authoritative information in regard to the subject matter covered. However, it is sold with the understanding that the publisher is not engaged in rendering legal or professional investment services. If legal advice or other expert assistance is required, a competent professional should be retained.

Table of Contents

Preface

Among the phrases that defined the 1980s is one that has relevance for people thinking about planning their retirement. The phrase made its rounds on coffee cups—at least that's where I read it first—and expressed the human condition in trying to wake up: "Life's a bitch, and then you die."

The purpose of this little book is to ameliorate that condition, at least as regards retirement and its planning.

Planning for retirement is, well, troublesome. It is sort of like what an English columnist once wrote about writing: Glorious in contemplation, hell in execution. You plan to put aside 10 percent of your income each year for retirement, and then you find yourself having to pay for new windows or a plumbing job. You plan for your investments to grow by 10 percent a year, and then the stocks you bought on your brother-in-law's advice in September drop 25 percent in October. As the saying goes, the best laid plans of mice and men often go awry.

So why plan? Well, so why live? Given the alternative, it's better. And the better you plan now, the better you live in retirement.

In writing, you need to have something to say and then a means of saying it; in retirement planning, you have to have a goal and a means of reaching it. You must know how you're spending before you can increase your savings. You must save before you can invest. You must know about investments before you can—and I apologize for these awful words—*maximize your income for retirement*. Three simple steps. That's what this book is about.

This book is not filled with grandiose schemes. It isn't written for economists or for professional investors. It's for the layperson. And it gets as practical as suggesting a weekly dinner menu. That's because it is the little things that add up. Sort of a reverse of the late Senator Everett Dirksen's comment about how government spending becomes so massive: "A million here, a million there. Soon it begins to add up to real money."

So this book will outline a way to define your retirement goal, to know how you spend your money, to increase your savings, and to invest so life in your retirement won't be foretold by a phrase on a coffee cup.

Duane D. Freese
October 1990

Introduction

You've heard it before: "It's just a matter of time." Unfortunately or fortunately, it's true. Today, you're working, trying to get ahead, doing something for your family. Tomorrow, you'll be retired—those golden years will be upon you. And what you do in those years depends on what you do now.

Sound gruesome? Something more to think about or fret over? Obviously, you *are* thinking (if not worrying) about it. You bought this book, or are at least reading this introduction. And you want me to tell you not to worry about it. That there's some simple way to handle your retirement. Tough.

If it was so simple, you wouldn't need a book. If it was so simple, all the advice you would need would be available on a three-by-five index card. This book is not a three-by-five index card. It is more like 200 of them.

There's a reason for the book being so long. Because the hard part of preparing for retirement is psychological. You need to be motivated—to get through the ERISAs, the IRAs, the REITs, the SS#s, the DRBs, and all the alphabet that people used to avoid by, well, dying early. You turn 65, or 70 and retire, and you're likely to live 15, 20, even 25 years. Modern health care, exercise, and diet all keep you cogent, capable, and carrying on longer than your forebears. That's nice, if you like life. But it's also a pain in the neck—you have to *plan* so you'll have some money for all those extra years.

You also need to understand how you, personally, deal with money. Not everyone handles his or her money the same way. Not everyone has the same goals, hopes, desires. And not everyone starts retirement planning in the same circumstances.

Different people are motivated by different forces. For some, it's reward; for others, fear. Most retirement planning books play on both of those. They scare the hell out of you about Social Security running out before you retire, your pension being unsafe, and the world being in a precarious state. Then they hit you with how you can become wealthy by taking on a bunch of tasks—managing apartments, or playing the stock market, or, horrors, doing both.

All of us would like to be rich. But going for the gold *strictly* for those golden years is foolish. For most of us, that would mean living so much for the future that *today* would be a wash. And what's the point of saving and investing if all it did was make our present life unrewarding?

But you can learn a valuable lesson from the grasshopper and the ant.

You know the story: The grasshopper plays and fiddles throughout the summer months while the hard-working ant labors to fill the larder for the cold winter ahead. The ant makes out fine, while the grasshopper is left freezing out in the cold. And in the woods they don't even have a warm grate.

Jimmy Carter's press secretary, Jody Powell, used that story to laud his president's energy policies when Carter was being challenged by Ted Kennedy for leadership of the Democrats in 1980. Political cartoonist Pat Oliphant drew Carter and Kennedy, dressed in the appropriate garb, for a stage play, with Carter remarking to scriptwriter Powell, "Did you have to make me *a damn ant?*"

Nobody wants to be an ant. It is much like being an economist, or an accountant. It doesn't ring of fun. It makes you feel a bit like one of an odd crowd. But, then, there is some safety in numbers. And there is some safety in saving. And, while it sounds like a cliche, you have to develop a saving habit.

Ants are creatures of instinct. You are a creature of habit. And the aim of this book is to teach you some tricks so savings become habitual, explain some things about saving and investing that may now seem scary or impenetrable to you, and, finally, to make saving as painless a process as possible.

First, though, you have to take stock of yourself. Whatever your personality—and most of us have a combination of characteristics—you can take more control over your money, and get more of what you want out of life, simply by doing a little planning. And this book will get you started.

How? Here are some of the questions that this book will help *you* answer:

1. When do you plan to retire and when will your spouse, if you have one, retire? How many years until you reach retirement?

2. What do you plan to do during retirement? Do you want to start a second career, a new business, be a teacher or consultant? Will you need to put money into that effort? Do you want to do volunteer work or perhaps pursue a hobby?

3. Do you plan to move to a new locale, and will you sell your home to do so? And if you move, do you plan to buy a bigger or smaller place?

4. What big-ticket expenses lie ahead? Do you have kids to put through college, or grandkids? Do you have family members you'd like to help buy a home? Do you have an invalid parent who may live with you?

5. What kind of insurance protection do you have for life, health, and home, and what will you need in the future?

6. How much income will you need to live on comfortably, without drastically changing your lifestyle?

7. How much Social Security income can you expect when you retire, and what about your health insurance?

8. How much will your employment or your private pension plan provide?

9. How much additional savings will you need to meet your retirement goal?

10. What kind of investments will be needed to get you through those golden years?

Some of those questions you can answer now. Some, you need some help to find answers for. And that's what this book is about. It can't do your investing for you. It can't change your personality. It can't get you a better job or ensure a wealthy retirement. But it can guide you to a course of action that will help you achieve what you want, and, it will even help you figure that out.

Before you move on to doing that, though, here's one thing to do now because you will need it later:

Call Social Security at 1-800-937-2000 and ask for Form SSA-7004 for both you and your spouse. The form is fairly simple. It asks for your last year's wages—money you earned while working, not your investment income, your current year's estimated wages, and what you expect to earn in the years ahead.

That later part is the only tricky part. How do you know what you'll earn? Don't worry. Happily, Social Security will figure that for you. They'll adjust your current wages by the average annual expected growth in wages. If you're expecting promotions, though, and think your wages will increase more than average wages, here's a formula for calculating that future value:

$$\text{Future value} = \text{Present value} \times (1 + i)^n$$

For example the future value of someone earning $30,000 today who expects 7 percent average increases in wages for the next 20 years would be:

$$\$30,000 \times (1 + 0.07)^{20} = \$116,090.53$$

You probably won't want to do that by hand. If you have a calculator with an exponent function, it's simple. For those who don't have such a calculator, you can use Table 1.1 to find a multiplier.

Just multiply your income by the multiplier for 5 percent if your career is established and by 7 percent if you expect future promotions, and you'll come

Table 1.1 Estimating Future Wages (Earnings)

Years to Retirement	5% Increase	7% Increase
5	1.28	1.4
6	1.34	1.5
7	1.41	1.61
8	1.48	1.72
9	1.55	1.84
10	1.63	1.97
11	1.71	2.10
12	1.80	2.25
13	1.89	2.41
14	1.98	2.58
15	2.08	2.76
16	2.18	2.95
17	2.29	3.16
18	2.41	3.38
19	2.53	3.62
20	2.65	3.87
25	3.39	5.43

to the income you can expect to earn the year before you retire. You can use this table and these multipliers to calculate the effect of inflation as well.

Within four weeks of sending the forms to the Social Security Administration, you will get back a report on the benefits you can expect at age 62 and at your full-retirement age, the benefits your survivors can expect, and the benefits if you become disabled.

You'll need that information later as you plan your retirement. So do that now.

Now, the fun part—getting started.

1

Where Are You?

Every game has rules. And the first rule of the retirement game is figuring out where you are. Financially. Physically, you could be in the tub, although that threatens to turn this book into a soggy mess. But I think it would be better if you weren't all wet while reading this section. In fact, it would be better if you were sitting with all your financial documents around you. Because that's what you're going to need. You have to draw up a budget.

Oh, bore, bore, bore. I know. It's the same reason that I put off doing my taxes. There's always something better to do—raking leaves, washing dishes, taking a nap, playing solitaire Vegas style. Unfortunately, there's no return in playing solitaire alone. I don't even get a refund. And the IRS isn't kind about a late return.

WHAT ARE YOUR INCOME AND EXPENSES?

I can't motivate you like the IRS can on taxes to get you to draw up a budget. But I can assure you that you won't get any return for your retirement until you do so.

Budgeting is boring, but it is also basic. It makes everything else easier. Like reading the rules of the game. To make your budgeting easier, here's a worksheet of what you need to know. Look through it and then I'll tell you how to fill it out.

Worksheet 1.1 My Personal Budget

	Per Week	Per Check	Per Month	Per Quarter	Per Year
EXPENSES:					
Shelter:					
Rent/Mortgage					
Property tax					
Condo fees					
Fire insurance					
Casualty insurance					
Heat/Air-conditioning					
Telephone					
Electricity					
Water					
Garbage pick up					
Maintenance					
Cleaning					
Garden supplies					
Subtotal					
Income taxes:					
Social Security					
Federal					
State					
Local					
Subtotal					
Transportation:					
Car payment(s) 1, 2					
Gasoline					
Maintenance					
Car wash					
License					
Insurance					
Public transport					
Tolls					
Parking					
Subtotal					
Food:					
Groceries					
Carry out/Restaurants					
Snacks (Yours)					

Continued

Worksheet 1.1 My Personal Budget, page 2

	Per Week	Per Check	Per Month	Per Quarter	Per Year
Food, Contd.:					
Snacks (Kids)					
Work lunches					
School lunches					
Subtotal					
Health:					
Medications					
Insurance					
Doctor fees					
Dentist					
Exercise classes/equipment					
Subtotal					
Education:					
Tuition					
Lessons					
Books/Supplies					
Subtotal					
Installment loans:					
Credit union (@ ___%)					
Credit card (@ ___%)					
Credit card (@ ___%)					
Department store (@ ___%)					
Student loan (@ ___%)					
Other (@ ___%)					
Other (@ ___%)					
Subtotal					
Clothing:					
Personal					
Spouse					
Children					
Repair					
Cleaning					
Subtotal					
Family:					
Life insurance					
Legal					
Child care					

Continued

Worksheet 1.1 My Personal Budget, page 3

	Per Week	Per Check	Per Month	Per Quarter	Per Year
Family, Contd.:					
Allowances	____	____	____	____	____
Gifts	____	____	____	____	____
Pet food	____	____	____	____	____
Pet medical	____	____	____	____	____
Other	____	____	____	____	____
Subtotal	════	════	════	════	════
Personal care:					
Hair (Adults)	____	____	____	____	____
Hair (Kids)	____	____	____	____	____
Toiletries (A)	____	____	____	____	____
Toiletries (K)	____	____	____	____	____
Postage	____	____	____	____	____
Tobacco	____	____	____	____	____
Alcohol	____	____	____	____	____
Other	____	____	____	____	____
Subtotal	════	════	════	════	════
Entertainment:					
Vacation #1	____	____	____	____	____
Vacation #2	____	____	____	____	____
Vacation #3	____	____	____	____	____
Vacation #4	____	____	____	____	____
Dining Out	____	____	____	____	____
Movies/Plays/Concerts	____	____	____	____	____
Sports tickets	____	____	____	____	____
Sports fees	____	____	____	____	____
Sports equipment	____	____	____	____	____
TV—Cable/Public	____	____	____	____	____
Clubs—Social/Country/Other	____	____	____	____	____
Subtotal	════	════	════	════	════
Donations:					
Religious	____	____	____	____	____
Political	____	____	____	____	____
Charitable	____	____	____	____	____
Other	____	____	____	____	____
Subtotal	════	════	════	════	════

Continued

Worksheet 1.1 My Personal Budget, page 4

	Per Week	Per Check	Per Month	Per Quarter	Per Year
Miscellaneous:					
Union and other dues	____	____	____	____	____
Unreimbursed business	____	____	____	____	____
Other	____	____	____	____	____
Other	____	____	____	____	____
Subtotal	====	====	====	====	====
Savings:					
Credit Union (@ ___%)	____	____	____	____	____
Bank (@ ___%)	____	____	____	____	____
Company plan (@ ___%)	____	____	____	____	____
IRA (@ ___%)	____	____	____	____	____
Keogh (@ ___%)	____	____	____	____	____
Stocks (@ ___%)	____	____	____	____	____
Bonds (@ ___%)	____	____	____	____	____
Other (@ ___%)	____	____	____	____	____
Subtotal	====	====	====	====	====
TOTAL EXPENSES:	====	====	====	====	====

	Per Week	Per Check	Per Month	Per Quarter	Per Year
INCOME:					
Paycheck	____	____	____	____	____
Paycheck	____	____	____	____	____
Subtotal	====	====	====	====	====
Dividends	____	____	____	____	____
Interest	____	____	____	____	____
Subtotal	====	====	====	====	====
Social Security	____	____	____	____	____
Pension	____	____	____	____	____
Subtotal	====	====	====	====	====
Gifts	____	____	____	____	____
Other	____	____	____	____	____
Subtotal	====	====	====	====	====
TOTAL INCOME:	====	====	====	====	====
NET INCOME:	====	====	====	====	====

[Net Income = Total Income – (Expenses – Savings)]

Ye gads! What are you getting into? Retirement planning has a tough set of rules just to get started. And a lot of details.

That's right. It does. But the details are important. And working out your budget is the first step, and biggest step, to saving for your retirement. And thinking about what it will be like. It puts you into the position of knowing a bit better not only where you are but where you'll have to be when you retire.

Look at where most of your income comes from now. Mostly from your paychecks. If you're like most Americans, dividends and interest, if any, are probably incidental.

Where will most of your income come from when you retire? If you're relying on Social Security and your pension, you should know this right from the start—they won't match your final year's earnings. Social Security will pick up about a third of your lost wages. Your pension, if you have one, may amount to a third. That's something you can check out with your employer. But remember this: Pensions don't necessarily increase after you retire. And inflation doesn't stop. That's why "living on a fixed income" is tough.

SAVING FOR YOUR FUTURE

Of course, you also lose some expenses. You won't be eating lunch at the office. You won't spend money on gas to go to work. Or for parking. If you have kids now, well, look at the big windfall you get when they are out of the home. School. Tuition. Student loans. Snacks. And, if you get them to call you, telephone bills! Look at the worksheet and you'll see what helping your children become self-sufficient can mean for your expenses.

Still, as a rule of thumb, you'll need about 73 percent of your last year's income to maintain your lifestyle. And you'll want that income to increase with inflation.

That's what retirement planning is all about: attaining a level of savings that will protect you against inflation. Writing down a detailed budget will help you generate those savings.

What are you looking for? Well, we don't expect you to become a *true* cheapskate. In California awards are given each year to people who find innovative ways to save money. For 1988, the winner was a man who took two-ply toilet paper rolls and separated them into one-ply rolls. He saved an amazing 22 cents a roll by doubling up. Another man unstitched his vacuum cleaner bags and emptied out the dirt. He would then sew them back up. (Hey, don't knock that idea. When emptying the bag one time, he found a penny!)

During the energy crunch of the 1970s, editorial writers were exhorting people to save every ounce of oil and gas and other energy source they could. Cut down, wear sweaters like Jimmy Carter, people were told. After writing a couple of editorials on the subject, I decided there were other strategies people weren't exploring. Such as? Well, don't just close off one unused room, make as many rooms as possible unusable by closing them off. Instead of an electric blanket, get a big woolly sheepdog or four or five Angora cats to sleep with. Or bundle the whole family together into one bed. And if you're not willing to take cold showers, shower together as a family. What could be better? You'd at least have somebody to wash your back.

I later found out that those ideas weren't so farfetched. Our pioneer families did much more. At proper inns in colonial days, five men would often share the same bed—sitting up because so many had consumption. And if you wanted a bath, well, you had to make sure you were either first or fourth or seventh in line because the servant who fetched the water would bring a fresh supply only after every third person. And that was in summer. In winter, nobody bathed. (And you wondered why spring cleaning was so important?)

No, you aren't expected to go to those extremes to achieve savings. Check each category on the expense portion. Except for the taxes, which you must pay, each "expense" has an element of choice. That's true even for tuition (there's always a less expensive school), groceries (you can pick cheaper cuts of meat), car payments (you can buy a cheaper car or a used car), utilities (yes, you can turn off your lights or turn down the heat or make sure the hot water is set at no more than 140 degrees F.). If you want to generate additional savings, work through the budget to decide what your priorities should be.

WITHHOLDING FROM UNCLE OR TO HAVE AND TO HOLD

You can generate additional savings even on the tax front.

For example, are you giving the government a free loan?

If you get a big refund each year, that's exactly what you're doing. A $1,000 refund means you are paying $83.33 a month more than Uncle Sam demands. If you had invested that money in a certificate of deposit (CD) or, better, assigned it to an individual retirement account (IRA) where it could earn tax-exempt interest, you'd have $1,064 in savings at the end of one year.

People overwithhold because they don't want to face penalties at the end of the year. That penalty amounts to about 10 percent of the difference between what you owe and what you pay.

But the penalty only goes into effect if you don't pay at least 90 percent of what you owe. So, there's a big cushion there. As long as you pay at least what you had to pay last year—after getting the refund back—you're likely to pay enough to avoid any penalty. Check your pay stub and check the amount that's being withheld. Then calculate it for the full year and compare it to what you owed last year. If you're paying a lot more and you or your spouse haven't gotten a huge raise, reduce your withholding. Don't pay Uncle Sam more than what's due.

Of course, some people actually count on big refunds for a major purchase or to add to savings. They're afraid if they got the money in each paycheck, they'd just spend it.

There's a simple way around that problem: When you reduce your withholding, arrange to automatically deposit the money in a savings account at a bank or credit union. Most employers will do that for you.

That way you don't have the money to spend, but Uncle Sam doesn't get it as a free loan.

This kind of nickel-and-dime savings may not be exciting, but it certainly adds up. And it helps make a habit out of saving. And that's what budgeting is all about—exposing old spending habits and developing some new savings habits.

INTEREST OF INTEREST

Look at your budget. How much interest are you paying each year?

Say you owe $2000 on your credit cards. Each year, that will cost you $200 to $235 at the 18 percent to 21 percent interest rates most credit cards charge. If you can't find a card that charges lower rates, you might consolidate your debts in a personal loan at a lower interest rate. That could save you about $80 a year.

What about car payments? For many people, a car is the second biggest investment they'll make. If you buy a $15,000 car, for example, at 12 percent interest over four years, your total payment will amount to $18,936. That's almost $1,000 a year in interest. After four years your car will be worth approximately $9,150—less than half what you paid for it. Final cost to you: $9,786.

If you bought a used car of the same make with moderate mileage for $13,361 at 12 percent for four years, you'd pay $16,867. The car would resell for $8,150, and your final cost would be $8,717.

Is it worth $1,000 for you to have a brand new car for one year?

Don't overlook hard-to-detect overspending on your grocery bill. Could it be made lower by buying some generic brands? Could you save something by putting leftovers into casseroles and soups? At $100 a week, a 5 percent savings in grocery bills amounts to $260 a year.

The point is, wherever you're paying a lot of money out, look for ways to save some of it. That's why you need to put your budget on paper, where you can see it. All of it.

Don't rely on your memory to tell you. You have to estimate some things, but you don't have to "guesstimate." It's a lousy way of showing you how you're behaving. We all have misconceptions about ourselves.

GETTING STARTED

To set up your budget right, you should spend a month gathering and marking down information. A month may sound like a lot of time, but you're trying to establish a habit. And it will take that much time to document your expenditures.

Gather as many of your past bills as you can find and screen them into the worksheet categories. Mortgage or rent payments are easy. So, too, should be tax payments (income tax forms and pay stubs provide plenty of information).

Utility bills are a little more difficult. You'll need a year's supply unless you're on a budget plan that evens out the billing over the year. A billing period while you're away on vacation doesn't give you a complete picture. A year's average, though, is a good sample. Just remember to adjust your average for any rate changes.

The toughest part is figuring out incidental expenses, from the groceries to the movies.

For those, you and the other members of your family need to get little budget books. Each of you should write out everything you buy each day for a month. Just like using a checkbook.

Establishing a family approach to planning is vital. Otherwise, the family's money manager will face continuous resistance and have to play the bad guy all the time.

That's not fair. It's also the cause of more family arguments, and more divorces, than any single thing. This amounts to conflicting money personalities.

Money can't substitute for love. Kids can get along with very little money, but they suffer greatly if they're given dollars instead of attention. Any parent who caves in to a child's demands for money rather than involving them in financial decisions or discussing the family's needs leaves them unprepared for adulthood.

Spouses who seem uninterested in the family finances, meanwhile, may only not want to seem ignorant. Financial information can be complicated. It can be overwhelming. But it doesn't have to be that way.

To explain to your family where the money is going, cash your paycheck and bring it home all in one-dollar bills. Then put it in piles according to what your expenses are. In a *USA Today* article, psychotherapist Olivia Mellan called this "shock treatment." It will not only wake up your family to the family's financial picture, it will do it in terms that everyone can understand.

That's also what carrying around the little budget books will do. It will make your spending understandable and focus your attention on what the family's paycheck is buying. Then all of you can decide whether what you're getting is worth it. And that's a big step toward not wasting money and having more for savings.

Dollars are made up of nickels and dimes and cents. A dollar a day is $365 a year. In just five years with investment in a 9 percent 90-day certificate of deposit, that would amount to $2,330. And we all can save a lot more than a dollar a day . . . with a little common cents.

So, start budgeting, and while you're doing that, go on to the next Chapter. We're going to show you what you're worth.

2

For What You're Worth

Your budget is your game plan, your tool to increase savings. But you also need a way to keep score, to find out where you are, what you've accomplished, and whether you're winning.

Most people have some idea of where they are. They can see that they own so many shares of stock or have so much in a savings account. They know they owe so much a month on a car or charge card and must pay so much a month for mortgage or rent. If they have homeowners' or renters' insurance, they may even have a rough idea about how much they'd expect to pay to replace their furnishings, their clothes, their television and stereo, among other things.

But most people don't know what they're worth—financially.

YOUR SCORECARD

The balance sheet—or net worth statement—fills that gap. It is your scorecard. It will tell you what you've accomplished and help you plot your savings and investment plan. It lets you know how much of your money is liquid—easily turned to cash—so you can get at it quickly in case of emergency. It gives you a picture of your liabilities—what you owe for your car, your home, your furnishings, your kid's education. It lets you know what you've accumulated—in goods such as cars and television sets, in real estate such as your home, in investments such as stocks and bonds.

Now, the tough part: You have to make up your own balance sheet, just as you had to put together your own budget. That's right. If you've finished most of your budget already, this means there is another set of forms to fill out and more information to gather.

That's probably why it's taken you such a long time to get started on a retirement plan. All the paperwork doesn't make it easy. But we all have to begin our voyage of financial self-discovery somewhere. That trip begins with finding out where you are—what you're worth.

Following is a sample balance sheet (Worksheet 2.1) for you to fill out. After you look it over, I'll explain what it means and what you have to do.

WORKSHEET 2.1 The Scorecard

BALANCE SHEET FOR: _____   DATE: _____

ASSETS		LIABILITIES	
Nonearning:		Current bills:	
Cash		Credit cards	
Cash on hand	____	Utilities	____
Checking account	____	Medical	____
Receivables:		Dental	____
Loans owed you	____	Other	____
Other	____	Installment debt:	
Personal property:		Charge accounts	____
House	____	Personal loans	____
Auto	____	Car loan	____
Property	____	Taxes owing:	
Jewelry	____	Income tax	____
Collectibles	____	Property tax	____
Furniture	____	Other	____
Earning:		Loans on investments:	
Saving account	____	Loans on investments	____
Real estate	____	Other loans	____
Stocks	____	Mortgage debt:	
Bonds	____	Home 1	____
Mutual funds	____	Home 2	____
Limited partnerships	____	Other	____
Other	____		
Pension and retirement plans:			
Life insurance			
Pension plan	____		
IRA	____		
Other	____		
Other	____		
Other	____		
TOTAL ASSETS:	____	TOTAL LIABILITIES:	____
NET WORTH:	____		

[Net Worth = Assets – Liabilities]

To people with any accounting background, this form holds no horrors. If you're one of them, then you probably can just skim the rest of this section, using it as a refresher. But if the form confuses you, don't worry, I'll happily walk you through the terminology and what it means for you and what it can do for you.

Assets

The balance sheet "balances" your assets with your liabilities, the difference between the two being your net worth. Assets are things you own. Liabilities are things you owe. It's that simple. If you owe more than you own, you have a negative net worth. If you own more than you owe, you have a positive net worth. Your assets always equal your liabilities plus your net worth.

Assets are split into different categories. The ones here have been split between those that are nonearning, that is they don't provide you a dividend or interest, and those that are earning, that is they provide you with income.

Cash in your pocket comes from your income; it doesn't earn you additional income unless you invest it. The same is true with a non-interest-bearing checking account. Cash and non-interest-bearing checking accounts are thus nonearning assets. They, along with securities that you can readily sell, also are often called current or convertible assets because you can quickly turn them into cash. If you have a lot of cash and a lot of other assets that you can sell on a moment's notice, you are liquid. If you lack liquidity, you are cash short or can suffer from a cash bind. More about that later.

One smart way to have some liquidity yet earn some extra income for yourself is to have a money market account. A money market account allows you to make out checks for free as long as you keep a minimum balance or set amount of cash in the account, typically $1,000 or $2,000. Usually, such accounts will provide interest based on your average balance or the minimum amount of money that was in the account at any time.

Because a money market account draws interest, it could be classified as an investment for that reason. But because interest on such accounts tends to be low and applied only to money you keep in the account, which you might remove at any time, you should think of it more like a checking account than an investment to provide you with steady income. As such, I'd recommend that you classify all but the minimum balance required for the account a nonearning asset, much like a checking account.

That's taking some liberties with the strict division between earning and nonearning assets, but consider your intentions. You don't intend your money market account as an investment for your retirement. It's a smart convenience—earning a little money while letting you write checks. Any money you make from a money market account should be viewed as a bonus that you can put into a real investment. In classifying your assets, keep in mind your intentions. It's the only way you can keep score on how you're meeting your financial goals.

After assets come receivables, your claims against another person or a company, usually for a specified dollar amount. For example, people often are paid weekly or biweekly, with the paycheck they get being for the week before. If you're in the middle of a pay period, they owe you for the time you've worked. You haven't gotten the money yet, so it is a receivable owed to you.

There are other receivables, too, that must be accounted for. You may have put down a deposit for a gas or electric meter, or for the receiver for your cable television, or for a lockbox, or, if you rent, as a security deposit for your apartment. This money is to be returned to you when you cease service, return the receiver, turn in your key, or turn back your apartment. You need to keep track of these items, and the receivables category is how you do that.

Loans payable to you, unless they are secured with collateral and have a set period for repayment, also should be considered as receivables. The loan payer may repay you at any time, which means it could earn nothing for you. And most personal loans people make aren't made for investment purposes but to help out a friend or family member. Applying the same rule as we did to money market checking accounts: Only if you intended the loan as an investment with the primary purpose of earning income from the loan should you classify it as an earning asset and an investment.

Receivables can be current if you can get cash for them quickly. (Turning in the apartment key or turning back your cable TV receiver to get the deposit back is easy. You also can expect to get your paycheck soon.) Receivables also can be noncurrent or fixed if they aren't easily converted to cash (moving out of your home or apartment to get a deposit back, for example, isn't easy); knowing the difference between the two types of receivables can help you determine how liquid you are.

Cash on hand, checking accounts, and receivables are easy to assign values to. With property, it's more difficult.

The worth of your personal property is its resale value now, *not* what you paid for it. What you paid for something is as irrelevant to determining its financial worth as your sentimental attachment to an old teddy bear would be if you tried to sell it. Its financial worth is only what somebody will pay for it.

Some assets appreciate, or increase, in value; others depreciate, or decrease, in value.

Often, but not always, your home and other real estate you own increase in value. How do you value real estate for your balance sheet? One quick way is by the assessed value assigned for property tax purposes. A caution here: Local governments often are inaccurate in their appraisals of property. It's to their benefit to assess it at a higher price, but they lack the time and the manpower to carefully appraise your home to determine its market value.

A better way is to check what homes in your area are selling for. Check a real estate guide or your local newspaper for home sales in your neighborhood. Find homes comparable to yours, then cut about 5 percent off the price to value your own. For a piece of land or other piece of property that isn't earning you income, do the same thing. Compare those items to the appraised value. If you find the government has appraised your property too high, protest at the next board of review hearing. After all, if they overvalue your property, it's costing you money—up to $45 for each $1,000 they've overvalued it in many jurisdictions. If they've undervalued it, you can tell them that, too. Or keep quiet and hope they don't notice.

To find the value of your car or boat—assets that decrease in value over time—check newspaper classified ads. They can provide you an approximate value. More exact values can be found from bluebooks at dealerships, but that isn't necessary. Values for used television sets, home computers, etc., can also be found in the classified ads.

For furniture other than antiques, you can check prices for similar pieces at used-furniture shops, which is the best way, or just depreciate it at about 15 percent for each year you've owned it until you reach its scrap value—what you'd value it at if you gave it to the Salvation Army. (Note: Most furniture sells at a tremendous markup when bought at retail furniture stores.)

For antiques, jewelry, and collectible items, such as art, coins, or stamps, the best thing is to have them appraised regularly. It's smart to do this for insurance purposes as well as for your balance sheet. You need to know what it would cost to replace them so they can be properly insured. You don't want to overpay; nor do you want to be underprotected.

Valuing your investments provides a different challenge.

Real estate you've invested in for rental income or other reasons will require checking newspapers for prices on comparable properties.

Current prices of stocks, bonds, and mutual funds can be checked in your local newspapers or a financial paper such as *The Wall Street Journal*.

If you own shares in a limited partnership, the current value can be obtained by calling any of several brokerage firms that buy and sell units on the resale (secondary) market. Some of them are:

- Liquidity Fund Investment Corp. (800-633-9090, 800-227-4688) in Emeryville, CA.

- Partnership Securities Exchange Inc. (415-763-5555) in Oakland, CA.

- Private Securities Network Inc. (415-456-8825) in San Rafael, CA.

- MacKenzie Securities (800-854-8357, 800-821-4252) in San Francisco, CA.

- Realty Repurchase Inc. (800-233-7357, 415-930-7001) in San Francisco, CA.

- Raymond James & Co. (800-237-7591, 800-248-8863) in Miami, FL.

- Equity Line Properties (800-331-9199, 305-662-4088) in Miami, FL.

- Investors Advantage Corp. (800-331-9199, 813-785-9566) in Palm Harbor, FL.

- Oppenheimer & Bigelow Management Inc. (800-431-7811, 212-599-0697) in NY.

For your retirement assets, the cash value of your life insurance—what you could get if you turned it in now—should be spelled out in your insurance company contract. If you can't find that, write your insurance company for a schedule of your policy's cash value.

If you have a company-paid pension or a profit-sharing plan, the personnel department should be able to tell you what that's worth. By law, you have a right to get an annual statement showing how much you've earned in retirement benefits, how much of it is vested (how much they are obliged to pay you), and when your pension will be 100 percent vested.

For a company-paid pension plan, you also should ask for both the Summary Plan Description (SPD), which is required under the Employee Retirement Income Security Act (ERISA), and a description of any changes since the last SPD. ERISA allows companies 210 days to update plans in the year after major changes were made, so the SPD by itself could be up to two years out of date. The SPD is important because it lets you know the future value of your pension.

If you have a 401(K) or other plan to which you contribute, its value will depend on the amount of your contributions and the value of the investments your company or you have made in the plan. Most plans are run by your company and, as with other pension plans, you can get the information on its current value from the personnel or pension department.

Your individual retirement account (IRA) also will be worth the value of the investments you've made with it. If you (or your spouse) are self-employed, your accountant should know what your Keogh plan is worth.

That sums up your assets and how to account for them. Doing so conservatively—without overappraising their worth while seeking the best estimate of their value—provides you with a cushion of protection. You know, don't count your chickens before they hatch. In valuing your assets, overcounting their worth makes you a cluck. You'll have to scratch around for a living if you pretend your nest egg is too big. So, whatever you own, value it realistically. It isn't what you think they're worth that matters. It is what others think. That's why you have to go to public sources of information—ads, stock listings, etc.—to find their value.

As a review of the main ideas we've talked about so far:

1. Assets are what you own.

2. Earning assets are assets that bring in income or will bring in future income—including stocks, bonds, limited partnerships, savings accounts, certain kinds of life insurance, the minimum balance of a money market account, rental property, pensions, IRAs, Keoghs.

3. Nonearning assets don't bring in additional income—cash on hand, checking accounts and money above the minimum balance of a money market account, nonrental property including your home, furniture, jewelry, collectibles, most receivables, your car, a boat.

4. Your liquidity depends on assets that either *are* cash or can quickly be converted to cash—checking and money market accounts, stocks, short-term receivables, the cash value of your life insurance, money in a savings account.

5. Your investments are those assets in which you've put money with the intent of making additional money from their future sale (collectibles, property not for rental or personal use, some stocks, some mutual funds) or from dividends and interest you receive (certificates of deposits, some stocks, bonds, rental property).

6. The value of your assets depends on what somebody else is likely to pay for them if they are put up for sale.

Liabilities

Account for your liabilities—they won't forgive you your debts.

Ben Franklin was wrong. There *is* something more certain in this world than death and taxes: *debt* and taxes. Somehow they both seem to mount up. No wonder that eminent American statesman John Randolph thought he had discovered the philosophers' stone that would turn everything into gold in the phrase "Pay as you go." By the time most of us pay what we owe, we (or the item we bought) is long gone.

The national debt is a reflection of our personal spending habits. The federal government's savings account—Social Security trust funds—mirrors our own savings rate of less than 3 percent of our nation's gross production. And our income doesn't match our debts any more than the federal government's does. Most of us owe somebody something—for our car, house, education, recreation vehicle, or vacation home.

Unlike the federal government, though, we have to pay off what we owe. Unlike the federal government, we plan to retire eventually.

Putting down our liabilities—our debts—in black and white can be a bit daunting, like looking up the face of Mt. Everest as we prepare our ascent. But just as building them up is so easy, so too is accounting for them. Unlike assets that you have to have appraised or read ads and price listings to evaluate, you have to do very little puzzling over what you owe people. For some reason, they are more than willing to tell you. They send you bills, they spell it out in contracts, they let you know exactly what you owe them. Isn't that nice of them?

Classifying your liabilities is another matter. Of major importance to you is distinguishing between short-term or current liabilities and long-term liabilities. In other words, what do you have to pay soon and what do you have some time to pay off?

For this balance sheet, I've grouped credit cards, utilities, medical and dental bills under current bills, or current liabilities. These are items you should pay off each month. The category "other" can be a plumbing or any other bill you must pay off in the next month. It also is your next car payment, house payment, tax payment if they must be paid within 30 days.

It's not hard to figure out that knowing your current liabilities is important. If you don't know what you have to pay *soon*, you may end up short of cash and short of credit in pretty short order.

YOUR QUICK CASH POSITION

One key to evaluating the health of a business is knowing its current position (or the current ratio). That means what current assets a business has to pay for its current liabilities. A 1-to-1 ratio of current assets to current liabilities is preferred because it means the business won't have to borrow to meet its monthly expenses. Borrowing is reserved for the purchase of major assets—machinery, buildings, etc.—not for paying postage, salaries, or installments on old debts.

You have to aim even higher, though. You have to make sure that your current assets exceed your current liabilities. That's the only way you'll generate any savings. To pay your on-going expenses, you shouldn't have to dip into your investments or sell your home, furniture, car, or the family jewels.

Therefore, although stocks and bonds, and some other investments are liquid, you shouldn't consider them current assets to use to pay your bills. Only your checking account, certain receivables, and money set aside in savings accounts intended to pay your bills should be counted as a current asset to balance against your current liabilities. We'll call those assets your "quick cash position."

Thus your quick balance would be:

[(Cash on Hand + Checking + Short-term Receivables + Designated Savings) – (Current Bills)] = Money for Savings or Money from Savings.

Balancing your quick cash against your current bills tells you part of your cash flow needs. The other part of your cash flow is a bit longer term. You will need money for your property taxes, insurance payments, or for any other major bill or loan due at a certain date. Recording the dates those items are due along with the amounts on your balance sheet will help you plan for them and set money aside either in a savings account or a certificate of deposit to meet those expenses.

That's the way to make your balance sheet work for you. Balancing your liabilities with earning assets to cover them and then using the interest income to increase your net worth by reinvesting it.

Notice that you do have something working for you to increase your net worth. If you own a home, the money you owe keeps going down with each house payment while the home's value should either remain steady or, in most cases, go up.

Don't let that deceive you. If your net worth is going up simply because the value of your home is increasing and the debt on your home is decreasing, you aren't generating additional savings. You're simply getting by. You can do better.

Look closely at your balance sheet. Over the next few years, you want to increase your earning assets and decrease your liabilities. Update the balance sheet every six months or so, paying special attention to the value of your investments and your long-term debts for home, furniture, and other major nonrecurring liabilities. You'll know you're gaining when your investments go up and your liabilities go down.

In the next Chapter, we'll tell you what you're shooting for.

3

Where Do You Go? Finding Your Rainbow

Now that you know where you are, it's about time you found out where you're going.

To some people, thinking about what lies ahead is depressing. When they look over their finances, they see some gigantic mountain of money that they have to climb to take care of their retirement.

Some financial planners like to make the mountain into Mt. Everest. One, for example, points out how a 40-year-old looking to have $135,000 in today's dollars by retirement time and counting on a 7 percent rate of return on his investment and a 20-year-life expectancy after retirement, would have to save $5 million over the next 25 years, or the equivalent of $80,000 a year. Why? Because of inflation. The planner envisions an average 5 percent increase in prices over that period.

That's impossible, most people are likely to feel, and throw up their hands and give up.

In fact, that scenario isn't as scary as the financial planner makes it. In fact, it's crazy.

People planning on that much income would have to have a lot of income to start with. At the time of retirement, they'd probably have about $650,000 in income. So, in the 10 years before they retire, they would be able to save an average of $100,000 a year, making up at a minimum $1.4 million of their retirement nest egg. The rate of return they'd get on their investments with a 5 percent inflation rate wouldn't be 7 percent, it would be closer to 8 percent. So, thanks to that wonderful thing called compound interest, they would have to invest only about 80 percent as much. They'd probably also have a home that would provide a huge capital gain at the time they retire—maybe as much as $2 million.

And they'd doubtless have some elaborate pension plan in which they could shelter a lot of their income from taxes and that would replace as much as half of their salary at the time they retire.

So, in reality, if they start saving 10 percent of their income in their 40s and 20 percent in their 50s, they'd be able to meet their retirement goals.

That's not as scary, or impressive, as the financial planner's scenario. Instead, it's realistic. You don't need to panic or fret. Just be realistic. Think. Then act.

Don't be frightened by inflation projections. Nobody *knows* what inflation is going to be. It could be 2 percent or it could be 10 percent. Through the early 1960s, it averaged under 2 percent. In the 1970s, it was about 10 percent. In the 1980s, it averaged around 5 percent. To assume that today's inflationary trend will be tomorrow's truth is also crazy.

If the inflation rate goes up, it's likely that your income, interest rates, and the value of what you own will go up, too. If the inflation rate goes down, your raises, interest rates, and the value of your assets will be lower as well.

That's why the information you've received from Social Security about your retirement is in current dollars. That's also why the pension information you've gotten is in current dollars. Social Security benefits are indexed to increase with inflation. And your pension, if you stay with your company, is indexed to increase with your salary, which is likely to rise with inflation.

Inflation will have an effect on your investments, on the choices you'll make between fixed return investments (such as bonds) and growth investments (such as stocks).

But don't be bullied by inflation projections into making super high-risk investments with possibilities of high returns, thinking that's the only way you'll ever raise enough retirement money. You're likely to lose your retirement nest egg that way.

And don't push the panic button and pour all your money into savings and investments, neglecting maintenance on your home or providing a decent education for your family—or more training for yourself. You'll shortchange your family and your future if you do.

Instead, act realistically and prudently.

First of all, set a goal for the income you think you need when you retire. And here's how you do that. Just answer the question:

Do you think you'd be satisfied living in retirement with the income you have now?

Sure, I know. I'd be a heck of a lot more satisfied with the income of King Farouk. But again, be realistic. If you feel strapped for cash now, you won't be able to increase your savings enough to live like a king later. You'll need to find ways to increase your income now—take an outside job, improve your skills so you can get a better paying position, have another family member take a job.

That's what I meant in the introduction about how you shouldn't plan to get rich for your retirement, do it now.

YOUR INCOME EQUIVALENT LEVEL

If you think you can "get by" with your current income, though, that provides the base for determining what you need to do to ensure an equivalent level of income in retirement.

To find that "equivalent level," we have to go back to the budget you've worked up to determine what you'll need.

With that as your guide, fill in the current year portion of Worksheet 3.1. It is almost exactly like the expense section on your budget, except that some categories are combined. That's so you'll *think* about how you're filling it out, rather than just going through the motions. (It also saves space.) After you've done that, I'll tell you how to calculate the rest of the form.

So, with your current expenses in front of you, now imagine what it will be like to be retired.

Housing

If you are buying a house and will pay it off by the time you retire, you can eliminate the mortgage as an expense. Even if you are still paying it off but plan to sell it, you most likely won't need as much space. So, you can reduce that by 30 percent. So, you can multiply what your paying now by 1, if you're paying rent or your mortgage isn't paid off and you don't plan to move to a smaller place. Or you can multiply by O if the mortgage is paid off. Or you can multiply it by 0.7 if you plan to move into a smaller home or apartment.

The rest of the items generally are decided by whether you move to a smaller place. One exception may be utilities. If you stay at home more, you'll probably use your lights, telephone, air conditioning, and heat more, so count on the costs for them increasing slightly.

Another exception may be your television, washer and dryer, dishwasher, garbage disposal, refrigerator, microwave and regular ovens, air-conditioners, and furnace. At some time during the 20 years after you retire, it is likely that one or more of them may need replacement. And those should be factored into your retirement cost, even though you may have them factored into your current budget as installment loans. How do you do that? Well, you take their cost and divide by 15, if you don't plan to live much beyond 85. If you do, pick any number. What do they cost?

Longer life and higher cost usually go together. So, too does greater capacity or power and cost. With those thoughts in mind, make a list of the home

---

WORKSHEET 3.1 Calculating the Equivalent Level of Income Needed

Expenses	Year	Current Factor	Retirement
HOUSING:			
Rent or mortgage	_____	0 or 0.7	_____
Property tax	_____	1.00 or 0.7	_____
Condo fees	_____	1.00	_____
Insurance	_____	1.00 or 0.8	_____
Utilities	_____	1.00 or 1.2	_____
Maintenance	_____	1.00 or 0.8	_____
Home furnishings	_____	0.5	_____
Other (e.g., appliances)	_____	see text	_____
HOUSING TOTAL:	══════		══════
TAXES:			
Social Security taxes	_____	0 or 0.5	_____
Income taxes	_____	0.7	_____
TAXES TOTAL:	══════		══════
TRANSPORTATION:			
Car payments	_____	see text	_____
Gasoline	_____	1.00	_____
Maintenance	_____	see text	_____
License	_____	see text	_____
Insurance	_____	see text	_____
Public transport	_____	0.5	_____
Other	_____	1.00	_____
TRANSPORTATION TOTAL:	══════		══════
FOOD:			
Groceries	_____	see text	_____
Carry Out	_____	see text	_____
Lunches	_____	0.5	_____
FOOD TOTAL:	══════		══════
HEALTH:			
Medications	_____	1.5	_____
Doctor	_____	1.5	_____
Dental	_____	1.00	_____
Exercise classes	_____	1.00	_____
Insurance	_____	see text	_____
HEALTH TOTAL:	══════		══════
EDUCATION:			
Education subtotal	_____	0	_____
EDUCATION TOTAL:	══════		══════

Continued

WORKSHEET 3.1 Calculating the Equivalent Level of Income Needed, page 2

Expenses	Year	Current Factor	Retirement
INSTALLMENT LOANS:			
Credit loans	___	0	___
Student loans	___	0	___
INSTALLMENT DEBT TOTAL:	═══		═══
CLOTHING:			
Clothes	___	0.75	___
Cleaning, repair, storage	___	0.5	___
CLOTHING TOTAL:	═══		═══
FAMILY MISCELLANEOUS:			
Life insurance	___	0 or 0.5	___
Legal fees	___	1.00	___
Child care	___	0	___
Allowances	___	0	___
Pet Food	___	1.00	___
Pet Medical	___	1.5	___
FAMILY MISC. TOTAL:	═══		═══
PERSONAL CARE:			
Personal care adult	___	0.8	___
Personal care child	___	0	___
PERSONAL CARE TOTAL:	═══		═══
ENTERTAINMENT:			
Vacations	___	see text	___
Other entertainment	___	see text	___
Television	___	1.00	___
Clubs	___	1.00	___
ENTERTAINMENT TOTAL:	═══		═══
DONATIONS/FEES:			
Donations	___	1.00	___
Fees	___	0	___
DONATIONS/FEES TOTAL:	═══		═══
MISCELLANEOUS TOTAL:	═══	1.00	═══
IRA, CD, BANK, PENSION:	___	see text	___
STOCKS, BONDS:	___	see text	___
SAVINGS TOTAL:	═══		═══
TOTAL EXPENSES:	═══		═══
INCOME:	═══		═══

utilities you own and then estimate their cost by looking for comparable items in a mail-order catalog or at an appliance store.

For example, my furnace isn't too big, but it's a top-of-the-line electric model and cost about $1,600. I also have two 6,000 BTU wall-unit air-conditioners worth about $500 total and one 10,000 BTU air-conditioner worth $600. My 40-gallon gas water heater is worth about $425. My electric washer and dryer are pretty cheap, so they are worth maybe $325. My gas range and oven are good and fairly large; they cost about $1,000. My refrigerator, with side freezer and ice maker, runs about $800. My dishwasher is a cheapy though; it costs about $400. And my disposal is a good one and cost $225.

I'll probably need either substantial overhaul or replacement of my furnace only once in retirement. The same is true for my range and oven and my refrigerator. That amounts to $3,400. My dishwasher, air-conditioners, disposal, water heater, and washer and dryer may need replacing twice. Add in a new TV, worth $700, and that's another $5,800.

The total is $9,200. Dividing that by 15, I'll need to set aside about $620 a year. (Yeah, I know it's $613.3333..., but I round up to the nearest $10, and so should you.) Put your own estimate into the other category on housing expenses.

Taxes

Unless one spouse continues to work, Social Security taxes disappear as an expense—you don't pay them once you retire. As for your income taxes, well, that depends on your income and what state you live in. If you make less when you retire, your taxes will go down. Even if you make the same amount, half of your Social Security benefit is currently untaxable. And some states grant tax exemptions to pension income. So, you are likely to pay only about 70 percent of what you're paying now. (I'll show you how to get greater savings later by certain kinds of tax-free investments.)

Transportation

You'd think your transportation expenses would go down in retirement, but they don't. You'll still need your car, and if you're married, your spouse will probably need a car, too, unless you plan to do everything together. Only if you have a third car for a child will you get any substantial savings. You can calculate that by simply eliminating the expense—on paper, not in reality, unless you want a big family fight—for that third car now. Commuting costs will be cancelled out by taking more trips for leisure, so don't count on saving money on gasoline and maintenance. Again, auto insurance will depend on how many drivers in your family will be covered at the time of retirement. If you have a teenage driver now, you'll get a big break when he or she grows up and moves out. Or, to put it more precisely, gains the wonderful freedom of being an adult.

Food

Your grocery bill will depend on how much of it now goes to take care of children. Once you no longer have to tell them that they have to eat all their veggies, you can stop cooking them and buying them. You won't have to pay for their snacks. So reduce your grocery bill by that amount. You also won't have to buy those three martini lunches at the office that the IRS folks were so worried about at one point. Tuna salad at home will be a nice and much cheaper alternative—up to $900 per working adult a year in savings. Unless, of course, you brown bagged it, like a lot people with kids, a mortgage, a house, and a dog. Then you know how cheap it is. And how healthy it is to eat light lunches, without all the grease, fat, and other things in many restaurant foods.

Health

This is where even if you stop paying for your kid's braces, you won't save a thing. In fact, you'll pay more. Medicare just doesn't cover as much as many people expect. There are high deductibles and, as of now, still some big gaps. They'll cost you between $500 and $2,000 a year to fill. And meanwhile, the years take their toll on you. So count on current medical costs to jump 50 percent. Add that increase and the insurance at $2,000. (Remember you want to be conservative in estimating your future costs so you'll save enough, and that means taking the highest probable cost, not the lowest.)

Education, Installment Debt

Unless you plan on getting a degree yourself, you should plan to enter retirement debt free, except for your home mortgage. If you have educational loans you've been paying for your youngsters, they can start picking up the tab. By retirement you will have accumulated most of the furniture and other major items you need. The one thing you might need money for is to replace home utilities, but if you follow the advice above, you'll have money on hand to do that.

Clothes

It doesn't take too much to figure out that your clothing bill will go down. No suits, if you're an office worker. No special work clothes, if you're a factory worker or carpenter or builder. Therefore, dry cleaning and laundry expenses will go down. The only problem is that you'll have more time to shop. That's why expenses in this catagory don't whittle down closer to zero.

Family Miscellaneous

Before you retire, you should take out insurance to cover the lost income or increased costs should either spouse die. But once you retire, you often don't need insurance to replace income. In retirement, much of your income comes from savings, which won't disappear if a spouse dies *if* you hold your assets jointly and leave a valid will. Another portion of retirement income is from Social Security, which provides a survivor's benefit as do many pension plans. So you will need either *no* life insurance or only enough to cover the loss of income from a pension that isn't passed on to a surviving spouse.

Your legal fees probably won't change. Periodically you might need to change your will or keep tabs on your investments, matters for which you'll need an attorney. So don't count on any savings there.

But you still have to feed the dog. For years your pet (or pets) provided you with warmth and comfort and, like you, may now require increased medical care. Now, it's your turn to repay all that loyalty and love and licks.

Personal Care

Presumably, you still will take baths or showers. Otherwise, you'll become that smelly old man or woman no grandkid wants to visit. Toothpaste, toothbrushes, mouthwash, Polident®, etc., are still in demand. So, why do I cut your personal care item to 0.8? No. It isn't that I think you'll take time to divide your two-ply toilet tissue to one-ply. It's my bet, though, that you won't get your haircut as often or won't go to the beauty parlor as much. Being elderly gives you a right—to look and to act as eccentric as you please. My father let his hair, what little he had of it, grow a little longer. It looked good, especially with the plaid shirt and polka dot pants and beret that he wore. Snappy takes on a whole new meaning when the only person you worry about impressing is yourself.

Entertainment

Well, there are different strokes for different folks. If in retirement you become a world traveler, or decide that now that you've got the time you'll get those $80-an-hour dance lessons, or that you'll play golf five days a week, you can spend a lot of money. Now that you do have the time, everyone has something that will fill your bill, although not necessarily your wallet or purse. Of course, you can take advantage of senior-citizen discounts. You could take up painting. That's cheap. And if you have children who join you, they may be able to pay their own way. If you have enough money, you might help them along; then they'll *really* enjoy seeing you. So, if you have kids now, count on your entertainment expenses staying about the same when you retire. If you don't, count on spending about 20 percent more. After all, having some fun is what retirement should be about.

Donations and Fees

Now that you got yours you're not going to help somebody else? Your causes were just for show? Nah. So plan to give as much in retirement as you do now. After all, the pleasure of giving and doing for others is more fun than rolling in dough. It's your way to leave a meaningful mark on the world. But, as for your union or association fees, you've paid your dues. Most don't require you to continue once you retire.

Savings

Obviously, you won't need to save as much when you retire as you should be saving now. But I don't know how much you're saving now. In fact, the rest of this book is devoted to how much you need to save for your retirement. Of course, you won't need to contribute more money to an IRA, or to a pension plan, or to any other retirement account. But don't take postretirement savings for granted. Only if your pension, Social Security, and your investments all increase with the rate of inflation could you get by for very long in retirement without lowering your living standard. So, rather than as a percent of what you're currently saving, add up your retirement expenses and multiply by 10 percent. That's how much you should add to your savings each year to keep the edge on your lifestyle and cut inflation's bite.

Your total current year expenses should equal your income. After all, they include your savings as well as what you spend. If they don't, ask yourself where that money went. But now you know what you need—in today's dollars—to retire. For most of you, your retirement expenses and income should come to about 70 percent of your current year expenses and income.

   You also should have a better idea of what your own retirement will be like. That's what this Chapter was supposed to do—focus your attention in some detail on what retirement is about and what you, personally, expect from it.

4

Insurance: How Much Do You Really Need?

Every time somebody mentions life insurance to me, I feel like breaking out in a rendition of my own version of the song "It's a Fine Life" from the musical hit of the early 1960s (boy, does that date me) *Oliver!*:

> *If you don't mind having to go without things,*
> *Buy insurance*
> Chorus: Buy insurance!
> *If diseased rats threaten to bring the plague in,*
> *Buy insurance*
> Chorus: Buy insurance!
> *Not for me a happy house, a happy retirement, happy life*
> *For when the time came to pay for them, I'd spent my money on premiums*
> *Buying, buying insurance!*

I'm not a big fan of insurance. It's one of those necessary evils that are a part of life—like death and taxes.

But necessary is necessary. And you may need some. The questions are, how much and what kind?

I don't think of insurance as an investment except in the broadest sense of the term. It is an investment to protect your other types of investments.

Think about it for a minute. If you were the beneficiary of an insurance policy, would you invest the money after the tragic event in insurance? Not unless your grief permanently scrambled your brains.

So, you don't put your money into insurance for what you'll get out of it. So, why spend any more on insurance than you absolutely have to?

The insurance industry will give you millions of reasons and millions of dangers that you should protect yourself against. They'll also tell you how good an investment cash-value or whole life or universal life or variable life or mixed-variable with annuity life or whatever they want to call it is.

The bottom line to you, though, should be to get the best coverage you can to meet your needs at the least cost possible. That way you'll have money to invest in real investments that really will make you money and that you don't have to die or get sick to get.

So how do you find out how to do that? The National Insurance Consumer Organization (NICO, 344 Commerce St., Alexandria, VA 22314, 703-549-8050) has a book, *How to Take a Bite Out of Life Insurance*, and it also publishes a convenient guide on insurance. They charge a $30 membership fee. But it can be money well spent if you are in the market for any kind of insurance, considering that differences on premiums for just an auto insurance policy can run into the hundreds of dollars. For life insurance, it's just more so. Another useful book is *The Individual Investor's Guide to Low-Load Insurance Products* (IPC, 625 N. Michigan Ave., Chicago, IL 60611). This book tells you how and where you can buy insurance wholesale.

I won't tell you what kind of insurance you should buy, but I *can* tell you what you need coverage for.

LIFE INSURANCE

If you have children or a spouse, you need some life insurance. How much? Well, that depends on your particular circumstance.

How many years does the mortgage on your house run? Are your kids' college educations paid for or do you have investments now to cover them? Does the other spouse have a job or the skills to get one? Did you perform a lot of home repairs or other domestic chores that may have to be paid for? How much of the pension will be passed on to the surviving spouse? Will your survivors continue to be covered by your employer-paid health care or will they have to buy coverage?

These are essential questions, and once you've answered them you can go over your budget and develop an estimate of what your loved ones will need in case of your death (see Worksheet 4.1).

That task is no different from what you did to determine your retirement needs. And the same principle you used to determine how much total investment you need for retirement can be applied here to determine how much life insurance you will need.

Example: Jane and John figured that their current expenses, not including savings, were $47,000 a year. Their continuing expenses would include their son's education, for which they had saved $10,000. He would need another $20,000, which they planned to borrow through a home-equity loan, adding

$2,400 per year to their $7,800 mortgage. John made $45,000; Jane, working part-time, made $12,000.

If John died, they figured a third of their food costs would go, along with his work expenses, his car payment and car insurance, Social Security taxes, and his membership fees. Vacation costs also would be cut. Because their son is over 14 they didn't add anything for child care, but they did figure that for Jane certain maintenance costs would increase, as John is a home-repair nut.

Shoving all these considerations into their budget they figured that continuing expenses without John around would amount to $41,000 even with the other costs. Jane figured that working full-time, she could make $22,000. But that would mean another $3,000 to replace her housework. The rest she would need to come from insurance that she could invest. John's insurance amounted to $90,000, and their noneducational savings totaled $35,000.

So, to replace John financially:

$$\$44,000 - 22,000 = \$22,000 + 0.07 \text{ Conservative Return on Investment} =$$
$$\$314,286 + \$50,000 + \$25,000 \text{ Funeral/Death Expenses} =$$
$$\$389,286 - \$90,000 \text{ Existing Insurance} =$$
$$\$299,286 \text{ Insurance Needed to Buy.}$$

Note, John and Jane also figured out a budget in case Jane died based upon their expense summary. Because Jane did all the cooking, cleaning, grocery shopping, and housework, ate less, had fewer membership fees, and also had a lower car insurance premium, the expense portion was reduced only to about $45,000, which matched John's salary of $45,000. However, they still had to cover savings, to which her salary contributed, so $50,000 was still needed. As far as funeral/death expenses they estimated $25,000. She had no employer-paid insurance, so they added a $75,000 rider on John's $300,000 policy to cover her death.

By working through your budget in a similar manner you can define your insurance needs precisely. But that doesn't tell you *what* kind of insurance you should buy.

Term insurance costs less, but it often won't give you coverage after the age of 65 except at extremely high premiums. Universal or whole life insurance costs more, but generally it won't drop your coverage after the age of 65.

To choose between term insurance or whole life, you need to understand the basic difference between term insurance and cash-value insurance, which goes under a variety of names (such as whole life, universal life, and total life).

Term insurance is pure insurance, which is why it costs less. Your premium pays for the benefit your loved ones will receive if you die.

WORKSHEET 4.1 Your Life Insurance Needs

	Current Expenses	Continuing Expenses
HOUSING EXPENSES:		
Mortgage/Rent	_____	_____
Home insurance	_____	_____
Fees	_____	_____
Utilities	_____	_____
Telephone	_____	_____
Garbage fees	_____	_____
Maintenance	_____	_____
Cleaning	_____	_____
Garden supplies	_____	_____
Subtotal	══════	══════
TAXES:		
Social Security	_____	_____
Income:		
Federal	_____	_____
State	_____	_____
Local	_____	_____
Subtotal	══════	══════
TRANSPORTATION:		
Car payments	_____	_____
Gasoline	_____	_____
Maintenance	_____	_____
Car wash	_____	_____
License	_____	_____
Insurance	_____	_____
Public transportation	_____	_____
Tolls	_____	_____
Parking	_____	_____
Subtotal	══════	══════
FOOD:		
Groceries	_____	_____
Take out	_____	_____
Snacks	_____	_____
Work	_____	_____
School	_____	_____
Subtotal	══════	══════
HEALTH:		
Medications	_____	_____
Insurance	_____	_____

Continued

WORKSHEET 4.1 Your Life Insurance Needs, page 2

	Current Expenses	Continuing Expenses
HEALTH, Contd.:		
Doctor's fees	___	___
Dentist	___	___
Exercise	___	___
Subtotal	___	___
EDUCATION:		
Tuition	___	___
Lessons	___	___
Supplies	___	___
Subtotal	___	___
INSTALLMENT LOANS:		
Subtotal	___	___
FAMILY:		
Life insurance	___	___
Legal	___	___
Child care	___	___
Allowances	___	___
Pets	___	___
Other	___	___
Subtotal	___	___
ENTERTAINMENT:		
Vacations	___	___
Dining out	___	___
Other	___	___
Subtotal	___	___
DONATIONS:		
Subtotal	___	___
TOTAL (without savings):	___	___
INCOME:		
Wages	___	___
Dividends, interest	___	___
Other	___	___
TOTAL	___	___
REPLACEMENT NEEDED:	___	___

Continuing Expenses – Continuing Income + 0.07 + the Greater of Noneducation Savings or $50,000 + $25,000 Burial Expenses = Base Insurance Needed – Insurance from Employer – Social Security Benefits (if any) = Amount of Insurance to Buy.

Cash-value life insurance, meanwhile, has a portion that goes to provide security to your survivors, with the rest of the premium going into a sort of savings component.

Thought of this way the issue is, what could you earn with the extra money you are paying for the savings component on term insurance? Could you make more investing that money in CDs or money market certificates or mutual funds or bonds?

That will depend on the return provided by the insurance policy. But you can't trust the insurance company to tell you straight out what that will be. Too often, they will give you figures that make the policy look good because such figures assume the insurer will do great things with your money.

For example, average returns on life insurance savings have been about 6.5 percent recently. Historically they run at only about 4 percent over a 20-year period. But if a company made 10 percent one year, it will imply that your savings in the policy will grow at that 10 percent rate over the life of the policy. That's unrealistic, and you should ask them to recompute projected returns at their average rate over the past 15 years.

Other companies will only mention in passing that if the cost of providing you the term portion of your insurance policy goes up—in other words, if they invested in a bunch of people who died ahead of their projections—they'll dip into the savings portion of your policy to make up the difference. Again, that would reduce your return.

Still other companies may front-end load their policies, giving you no cash value for the policy in the first few years, then increasing it only gradually. Basically, with those policies, you're paying a supper high premium for term insurance until your cash value actually builds up.

That's why term insurance often makes more sense, especially if you're under 45. It gives you the most bang for the buck. And if your conscientious enough to save and invest the difference between your premium for term and what it would be for a comparable whole life policy, you can make your retirement nest egg grow much faster, and better.

Only if you aren't willing to do your own saving is a whole-life policy likely to be a really good buy for you. Because then it will force you to save money you would spend otherwise.

If you've already "invested" in a whole-life policy and don't have many years to go to pay it off, don't just get rid of it. Check it out and compare what other insurance is available. And get some expert advice, such as that in the NICO guide to life insurance mentioned on page 36.

The basic rules are simple: Don't get more insurance than is needed to replace your income. If possible, look at your expenses and determine if you actually need less. If additional coverage is available through where you work, that may be the cheapest way to add to your life insurance coverage. When you get to age 65, drop most of your insurance. Get only enough to cover funeral expenses and a 70 percent portion of any decrease in your pension.

And rule number 1: Don't scrimp on your savings to buy unnecessary coverage—it won't pay off in the long run, and you can't take it with you.

HEALTH CARE INSURANCE

One of the biggest costs that could wipe you out in old age is for long-term care, whether in a nursing home or at home with nursing care.

Experts estimate that retirees in the year 2000 will need $50,000 to $200,000 in savings to pay for long-term care. Brookings Institution estimates that in 2020, a year in a nursing home will run $158,000. Costs for long-term care now run $20,000 a year.

What about Medicare? Well, Medicare doesn't cover long-term care. It, along with physicians' fees, are the big gaps in Medicare coverage. And if your employer's insurance won't extend to cover it, you'll have to.

The question is whether you should try to do it with your personal savings or through private insurance. That question can be answered by how much each of them costs.

To cover the cost of long-term care personally, is simply a matter of mathematics: $200 invested each year for 15 years at 7 percent interest will raise about $5,000, over 20 years it will raise about $7,900, and over 25 years it will raise about $11,700. So, if you invested $2,000 a year for 15 years, or $1,260 a year over 15 years, or $860 a year over 25 years, you could cover the minimum cost of a nursing home at the time you retired without losing income. And on the 75 percent chance that you won't go to a nursing home, you'll have that money to cushion your retirement.

Sounds like a good deal. But insurance, by working on those same odds, can give you a good deal, too. If you're in good health, you can get protection against that one-in-four chance you will end up in a nursing home for $140 a year at age 40, for $250 to $300 a year at age 50. And that's inexpensive protection for such a high risk. What you should look for:

- A policy that provides for noncustodial as well as custodial or nursing home care. Often, the nursing home is followed by home convalescence, but you'll need nurses and other help to get through. A policy that covers only nursing home care will leave you relying on your own resources if you need home care instead.

- A policy that increases its per-day payout with the inflation in nursing home care. One that covers actual costs less a deductible would be even better. You can get a cheap policy that's worthless to you if it doesn't, as the cost projections for nursing home care show.

- A policy that doesn't require hospitalization first. Most people entering nursing homes never were cared for in a hospital.

- A policy written by a financially secure company. A new company or one that has few financial resources to draw from could go bankrupt quickly leaving you with no coverage.

- A policy that is convertible to other uses or will provide you some return of the premiums you've invested over time if Congress approves federal financing of long-term care. Then the money spent won't have been money wasted, but can save you with other health-care needs. And only insurance companies looking to gouge consumers rather than meet needs won't provide some kind of alternative. After all, they'll have built up substantial reserves to meet claims that won't exist if the federal government takes over.

- A policy that is automatically renewable as long as you pay your premiums. That's automatic. You don't want them to be able to cut you off after years of paying just when you reach the age at which you're most likely to need the coverage.

By asking these questions of an independent insurance agent, you'll be able to find coverage to protect your health and your wealth. And that's wise.

OTHER INSURANCE

The net worth statement you developed earlier provides you a sure method of determining how much coverage you need for your homeowners', fire, and auto insurance for replacement costs. Most people either overinsure or underinsure their assets. You can't afford to do the former, because it takes away from your savings. You don't want to do the latter, because it opens you up to new risk. You want your insurance to be just right—so use the information from your net worth statement to determine whether your coverage is appropriate.

And once you've settled all your insurance needs, get busy paying the premiums on your biggest insurance policy—that for your retirement.

5

What Have You Got To Get There? Your Not-So-Fixed Income

So, how much do you need to save for your retirement? In Chapter 3 you learned how much retirement income you'll need to maintain your current lifestyle without making too many adjustments. To meet your retirement expenses, including savings as a hedge against inflation, you found you probably won't need as much as you do now. But to supplement that amount simply from savings you've set aside would leave you with a big nest egg to create, especially if you don't have much in savings now.

For example, let's say you're making $40,000 now and your expenses at retirement will amount to about 75 percent of that. That's $30,000 a year in today's dollars that you'd need from your investments without any other sources of income. That would mean you'd need $500,000 in today's dollars if your investments earned 6 percent interest, and $375,000 if they earned 8 percent. That's a big chunk of change, especially since you will have to add even larger amounts to cover the effect of inflation. Using the Future Value formula (see Introduction), you would need $500,000 x (1 + the inflation rate) exponentially increased by the number of years until retirement.

You can compute what it would take to meet your own goal the same way. Simply divide your retirement income goal by 0.06 and by 0.08, the high and low rates of return you might expect on your investments at retirement assuming historical rates of return continue:

Retirement Income Goal ($) + 0.06 = High Savings Equivalent

Retirement Income Goal ($) + 0.08 = Low Savings Equivalent

Now, using the future value chart in the Introduction, multiply the high savings equivalent times the 5 percent multiplier and the low savings equivalent times the 7 percent multiplier for the number of years until you expect to retire. (That's not a misprint. If your return on savings is low, it will be because inflation was low. If it was high, it will be because inflation was high. Simple economics. So, that's why you multiply the high savings equivalent by the low inflation rate, and vice versa):

High Savings Equivalent ($) x 5% = Savings Adjusted for 5 percent Inflation

Low Savings Equivalent ($) x 7% = Savings Adjusted for 7 percent Inflation

Looks pretty discouraging doesn't it? But don't let it be. Remember inflation also boosts your income. And if you own your own home, you could have a lot more money to put into savings.

I think of this as a law of relativity for personal finances. Inflation doesn't occur in a vacuum. Other things happen so that people adjust. The hard part for most people is that they see the inflation-changed figures and don't take into account the other adjustments. They aren't actuaries. That's why I am emphasizing for the moment that you think in current dollars, rather than focus on the paper mountain created by inflation.

Part of the personal finance law of relativity is that the law of the land is working for you. It's measured in your Social Security benefits and in the savings you can accumulate in pension or personal retirement plans.

What you really need to save for retirement must take those hard-earned assets into account. To help you do so, I've created Worksheet 5.1. As the immortal Jimmy Durante said, "I got a million of them."

To fill out this retirement savings form, just write in the figures that you secured from Social Security, or from your company benefits office, or from your actuary. The revenue portion of the personal budget you filled out in Chapter 1 contains current investment income information. You can fill it out using the information from the savings portion of your budget, the information provided you by Social Security and your company benefits office or your private actuary and the income goal you set for yourself in the previous chapter.

Now you know where you've got to go—how much, in today's dollars, you must save. But before we go on to discover how to get there, you should first know something about that big portion of your retirement savings you are counting on—your Social Security and your retirement plan.

SOCIAL SECURITY

For people with incomes from $10,000 to $30,000, Social Security is often the single largest contributor to their retirement income. And whatever your income,

---

WORKSHEET 5.1 Retirement Savings

Social Security		$_____
plus Pension	+	$_____
Subtotal:		$_____
plus Private Retirement Plan	+	$_____
Subtotal:		$_____
plus Current Investment Income	+	$_____
Available Retirement Income	=	$_____
Retirement Income Goal		$_____
minus Available Retirement Income	–	$_____
Future Income Needed	=	$_____
Future Income Needed		$_____
divided by High Return	÷	0.08
Low Amount to be Saved	=	$_____
Future Income Needed		$_____
divided by Low Return	÷	0.06
High Amount to be Saved	=	$_____

Social Security will contribute more than small change. It had better. It's taking a big chunk of change from your income now.

To become eligible for Social Security, a person must have worked 40 quarters, or 10 years, earning a minimum of $470 per quarter in 1988 dollars. But Social Security isn't just for retirement. If you die tomorrow, your family gets a death benefit if you accumulated at least six quarters of earnings in the last 13 quarters. That includes $255 for funeral expenses and benefits for a spouse caring for a child under age 16 or for a child under age 18 equal to 75 percent of what your retirement benefit would have been. In addition, your spouse will receive 100 percent of your retirement benefit when she turns 65.

Some critics of Social Security say that you should worry less about survivor benefits than about the survival of Social Security. Pointing to the baby boom and actuarial projections, they claim Social Security may not be there by the time those now in their 30s retire. Or, they argue, the benefits will be so reduced they won't be worth anything.

Baloney. Politics is politics. And no politician is going to kill something that will bring a horde of the most active voters into the booth with a single purpose in mind—keeping their retirement checks. And the same thing that is a problem for Social Security—the baby boom generation—is the same thing that will make Social Security even more sacrosanct. More voters. There are 2.7 million people over the age of 85 in the United States today. There'll be 5.4

million by the year 2010. One in seven people in the United States will be over the age 65 in 2010, and one in four will be over the age of 55. That's a big block of voters to outrage.

Does that mean there will be no adjustments in Social Security? No. Some adjustments will be made. Already, the age for becoming eligible for full Social Security benefits has been raised, rising to 67 for people born after 1960. Table 5.1 shows the Social Security Administration schedule.

TABLE 5.1 Social Security Age Eligibility

Year of Birth	Full Benefits
1937	65 years
1938	65 years, 2 months
1939	65 years, 4 months
1940	65 years, 6 months
1941	65 years, 8 months
1942	65 years, 10 months
1943–1954	66 years, 0 months
1955	66 years, 2 months
1956	66 years, 4 months
1957	66 years, 6 months
1958	66 years, 8 months
1959	66 years, 10 months
1960 and after	67 years, 0 months

In addition, the early retirement benefit is going down—from 80 percent of the full benefit if you quit at age 62 to 70 percent.

And Social Security taxes are rising, both on the amount of income subject to the tax and the rate (see Table 5.2).

Those changes make sense, no matter how much you might yearn for carefree days in sunny climes or a lower tax bill to let you get there sooner.

The changes will create a $12 trillion reserve by 2030, and by then it'll be needed to handle the baby boom. To handle the fact that we're living longer.

At the turn of the century the likelihood that a person born in 1990 would survive until age 65 was just 40.9 percent; the chances of reaching 85 years of age was only 6.1 percent. Indeed, the life expectancy at age 45 of a person born in 1900 was only 69.8 years of age.

A person born in 1950 has a 67.6 percent chance of reaching age 65 and a 15.8 percent chance of reaching the age of 85. And a person born in 1950 who

TABLE 5.2 Social Security Tax Rates

Year	Top Wage Base	Tax Rates	Maximum Tax
		Employees	
1988	$45,000	7.51%	$3,380
1989	48,000	7.51	3,605
1990 (est.)	50,100	7.65	3,833
		Self-employed	
1988	45,000	13.02	5,859
1989	48,000	13.02	6,250
1990 (est.)	50,100	15.3	7,665

reaches the age of 45 can expect to live until they're 71.6 years of age. Both the person born in 1900 and the person born in 1950, even with the higher retirement age, will have about the same number of years of receiving full retirement benefits. And for people born after 1950, their life expectancies are higher still.

So, live longer, work longer. As the head of the Gray Panthers, Maggie Kuhn, at age of 84, told me: "Retirement can be fatal." She wants to set up child-care centers in every retirement home and community which she thinks are now "playpens for wrinkled babies," so retirees can still contribute their wisdom and also be more active. That way they can live longer. Besides, the higher retirement age gives you more years to save for retirement.

Still, what can you count on from Social Security? Well, not all you need. Social Security is the floor of your nest, not the walls and roof that you want so you can live comfortably.

Social Security won't replace all of your lost wages. And it replaces less and less as you make more and more. Indeed it's going back to its original role, rather than moving on from what it expanded into in the 1960s and 1970s.

When Social Security began in the late 1930s, it provided at most a third of a retiree's income. And not for very long because most people didn't live much beyond 63. But that changed. Poverty among the old became an issue in the Great Society years, and Congress increased Social Security benefits in big chunks. That nearly bankrupted the pay-as-you-go system. And with the baby boom looming, Congress in the late 1970s moved to reduce benefits for new retirees beginning in the early 1980s. The result of all that activity can be seen in the Social Security Administration table on average earnings replaced by Social Security for single workers (see Table 5.3).

**TABLE 5.3 Average Earnings Replaced by
Social Security for a Single Worker**

Year	Percent Income Replaced
1950	30%
1958	34
1967	36
1975	56
1983	46
1986	41

We can expect that trend to continue because workers' earnings are expected to rise faster than inflation while Social Security will increase at no more than the rate of inflation. That shouldn't discourage you, though, because if your income rises faster than the cost of living, you have more money to save and won't need as much from Social Security.

And it shouldn't discourage you, either, that the earnings replaced by Social Security decline as your income goes up. Table 5.4 shows the Social Security Administration's schedule for wage replacement for retirees in 1988.

As you can see, Social Security replaced more of a low-wage worker's income than a high-wage worker's income, providing an additional 50 percent for a dependent spouse.

That may not seem fair. After all the single worker may have paid as much in taxes as the couple. And the higher-income worker paid more than the

TABLE 5.4 Wage Replacement for Retirees, 1988

Salary	Salary Replaced	
	Single Worker	With Dependent Spouse
$12,000	46%	69%
18,000	40	60
35,000	28	42
45,000	22	33
55,000	18	27
100,000	10	15

lower-income worker (although anyone in 1990 making $50,100 and more paid the same amount). So why aren't replacement ratios more equal? Because Social Security is social insurance. It's meant to provide for the needs of the poorest not make things cushy for the more well-to-do. That may not seem fair to some, but the alternatives—old folks eating dog food and bag ladies going after garbage—aren't appetizing either.

There is, though, an odd component to Social Security that makes it seem almost "anti-social." Two-earner couples are the norm today rather than the exception as in the past. Husbands and wives both are kicking in large sums into the Social Security coffers and are eligible for earned benefits—but not necessarily equal to what each would get as single workers.

In 1988, a single worker who earned at or near Social Security's earnings cap for 35 years was eligible for a benefit of $10,056. Two unmarried individuals who shared a home, named each other sole beneficiary in each other's wills, signed a partnership deed for all property would get $20,112. If the couple were married, though, they'd get a maximum benefit of $17,598—$2,514 less.

Another odd "married" penalty has to do with the income tax. The government will tax up to half of the benefits of a married couple filing a joint return if their adjusted gross income, tax-exempt income, and half their annual Social Security payments combined exceed $32,000. If you're single, those things must exceed $25,000. An unmarried couple could earn $50,000 before they have to pay income tax on extra benefits. Even taking into account the tax advantages married couples receive filing jointly, there is a tax penalty for being a married two-earner couple prior to retirement.

I guess what the government is trying to tell you is that two bound in "holy matrimony" can live more cheaply than two "living in sin." But your concern is not marital equity but what you can count on. And what you can count on is your Form SSA-7004, which you can slug into your retirement plan. For most of you reading this book, that should amount to about 15 percent to 30 percent of your pre-retirement income.

RETIREMENT AND PENSION PLANS

So, Uncle Sam isn't going to play rich uncle and support you through your retirement. What about your own rich uncle—the company that employs you or the business that puts bread on your table and in your bank? How is it handling your retirement needs?

Information provided by your employer or your private self-employment plan (via investment advisor) gives you the bottom line of what you can expect out of those vehicles.

But they count on your spending a good deal of time with your company. Years and years, as a matter of fact. And the longer you work for a single company, the more you can expect.

According to the Employee Benefit Research Institute, the typical monthly pension of a worker earning $40,000 the year before retirement in 1988 is shown in Table 5.5.

TABLE 5.5 Pension for $40,000-a-Year Worker

Years with Company	Average Monthly Benefit	Average Yearly Benefit
10	$326	$3,912
15	479	5,748
20	623	7,476
25	760	9,120
30	886	10,632
35	988	11,856
40	1,075	12,900

The "average" runs from less than 10 percent of a worker's pre-retirement income to just under 33 percent. For a 30-year employee, it's 26 percent. But you have to remember this about averages: People have drowned in lakes with an "average" depth of two feet.

Not knowing how your pension or retirement plan works can leave you foundering far from a safe retirement shore, the life jacket of a pension too small to support your weight.

It's better you understand now how your company or self-created retirement plan works, rather than after when it's too late to add extra flotation devices.

Employers often speak in glowing terms of what they're giving you. But it isn't their life if you end up over your head; thanks to federal law, you have more choices in regard to pension plans than you did before.

There are two basic retirement plans—corporate or company programs and private plans.

Of more than 40 million Americans covered by corporate plans, more than 28 million are covered by defined benefit plans. An increasing number, now 12 million, are taken care of by defined contribution plans.

Defined benefit plans set a benefit that the company will pay to you upon retirement. The fund is pooled, without a distinct account for each person.

Defined contribution plans require employer contributions that are based on some kind of formula, company profit, or some other measure. Each plan participant has an account that grows with new contributions, investments, and accrued interest.

Do you get the difference?

In a defined contribution plan, there is no guaranteed return. The benefit you get at retirement depends upon the contribution made by your company each year plus the interest, dividends, and increase in the value of investments. The contribution formula is set, not the benefit.

In a defined benefit plan, you get a guaranteed return for your years of service. The company's contribution can be anything needed to meet the promised benefit formula. But the formula for determining your benefit—years of service, average salary—is set.

In both types of plans, one key thing is the vesting formula. Vesting is simply your right to a benefit. Under the 1986 Tax Reform Act, as of 1989 there are only two types of vesting allowed for pension plans.

The first type provides full vesting of benefits in the fifth year of the plan. A plan year is not necessarilly January to December but can be any 12-month financial year for the plan itself—June 1 to May 31, April 1 to March 31, or whatever. Companies often set plan years according to their manufacturing and selling cycles.

The second type gradually vests you over seven years, with no rights for the first two years, 20 percent vesting in the third year, 40 percent in the fourth year, 60 percent in the fifth year, 80 percent in the sixth year, and 100 percent in the seventh year.

Who benefits most from different kinds of plans and what their risks are will be covered in the following sections.

Defined Contribution Plans

For employees who switch jobs often, the defined contribution plan is best. The reason is simple—usually, they can carry the contributions with them, whether it's a profit sharing arrangement or a thrift or savings plan.

Profit Sharing. Under a profit-sharing plan, the company puts a designated amount (devised by formula) into each of the accounts for employees participating in the plan. The company, or its chosen intermediary, then invests the money. The fund increases with each successive contribution and with the income from investments.

Some profit-sharing plans require vesting. If you quit before attaining that right, the money in your account is split up among the other plan participants.

So, what you need to know about a profit-sharing plan is:

1. The vesting period, if any, and what happens when you quit or are fired. Even if you aren't fully vested, you should be able to take whatever is in your account with you. But you should make sure. Some plans require that you keep the money in your account and allow you to withdraw it only after retirement. If you do get a lump sum payment for your account when you leave, then you have three choices. You may choose to spend it, but then you must pay Uncle Sam a 10 percent penalty. After all, the only reason you don't pay taxes on interest and contributions to the profit-sharing plan is because Uncle Sam has set retirement savings as a socially desirable goal. Secondly, you can roll it over into an Individual Retirement Account or into another company's retirement plan without a tax penalty. Or, thirdly, if the lump sum payment exceeds $3,500, you can require that the company leave it in your account. By law, your soon-to-be former employer has to get your written permission, and that of your spouse, to cash out your retirement plan if it's worth more than $3,500.

2. The date at which benefits are earned for any plan year is especially important if you're considering a job change. If you have only a little time until the vesting date or the earnings date for a contribution, you might hold off leaving.

3. The formula for splitting shares to the plan. Usually, it is based upon salary. For example, if your salary is equal to 1 percent of the company's payroll, you get 1 percent of the amount contributed to the profit-sharing plan. Sometimes, though, higher-paid members get more.

4. The kind of investments for the plan. Because benefits from a profit-sharing plan depend on the success of their investments, you will want to make sure you don't duplicate its mix of investments with your own. The reason is as simple as not putting too many eggs in a single basket—you can defray risk through diversification. I'll discuss that more fully later. But knowing how your profit-sharing plan is invested will help you diversify your other, personal investments for retirement.

    For example, some profit-sharing plans pay off in company stock. They are known as Employee Stock Ownership Plans or ESOPs. In them, the employees get shares of company stock—the number of shares is based on their salaries—put into a retirement account. Dividends from the stock are added to the account.

    The problem with ESOPs is that their success and worth depend upon the company's success, and usually you can't diversify your holdings or sell your stock until you leave the company. That really puts all your eggs in one basket and puts you at great risk of losing retirement benefits if the company runs into trouble.

For example, if a company creates an ESOP as a guard against a hostile takeover, it is piling up debt to create the ESOP, which will depress its stock price later.

The key question about an ESOP is this: Can you sell off part of your stock to diversify your retirement plan? If you can't, then it's essential to invest as much of your other money in other kinds of investments to spread and reduce your risk.

Some companies, recognizing the risk to employees in profit-sharing plans, also allow employees to put money into another plan called, because of its tax code reference, a 401(K) plan.

It isn't hard to understand why 401(K) plans are becoming very popular. They:

1. Provide a big tax deduction, up to $7,700 in 1989. You don't pay taxes on that income or on the money your contributions earn until you withdraw it. And then you can take advantage of 5-year averaging, which normally means a lower income tax rate. Early withdrawal prior to 59½ years of age carries a 10 percent penalty tax, except for hardship cases.

2. Allow matching contributions. Eighty-five percent of companies with 401(K) plans usually put up 50 cents for each dollar you invest in the plan, up to 6 percent of your income.

3. Have flexibility. Most provide a range of options from which you can choose, including investment in stocks, in bonds, in money-market funds. That lets you tailor your plan to your entire retirement portfolio, diversifying your investments to reduce risks and take advantage of all kinds of opportunities.

401(K) plans have some drawbacks. The IRS is toughening provisions for hardship withdrawals and for loans against 401(K) accounts. Due to federal regulations lower-paid workers in 401(K) companies put in nearly as much as higher-paid workers. If they don't, the company must limit the amount of tax deductible income you put in. Despite these shortcomings, 401(K) plans are a good way to boost your retirement savings.

Other types of defined contribution plans include Cash Balance (or Account Balance, or Cash Account, or some infinite variation thereof), Money Purchase (a hot item for people without a Cash Balance), and Simplified Employee Pension (which is so "simple" it will need explanation).

Cash Balance. A set percentage of a participant's salary is contributed by the company to an individual account where it earns a specified rate of interest tied to the inflation rate or the federal Treasury bill rate. The rate usually is below what the funds contributed by your company to the account actually earn, and the company keeps the difference. This makes it less expensive than many other plans and potentially less lucrative to you, unless your company reinvests some of the savings.

Money Purchase. Again, a set percentage of a participant's salary (up to 25 percent if employed in an incorporated business or 20 percent if self-employed or a member of a partnership)—but no more than $30,000 a year—is contributed to an individual's account. If an employee leaves the company before being fully vested, the corporate contributions to the fund are reduced by the amount forfeited by the participant. A vested participant gets the money in the account as would occur at retirement. Annual investment earnings and losses are added to or subtracted from the account balances.

Simplified Employee Pension. SEPs were created by the Revenue Act of 1978. Under a SEP, an employer can contribute up to 15 percent of an employee's salary, but no more than $30,000, into an IRA. What makes the plan different from most other plans is that an employee is immediately vested for the amount put into the SEP account. As with other retirement plans, employees can't withdraw before age 59½ without incurring a penalty. The cost of the benefit is deductible to the company and not taxed to the employee.

Whichever type of defined contribution plan you have, the key questions remain the same:

What is the formula for contributions? Will it rise with your income or will it depend on company profits?

What are the contributions invested in? Are they split among a variety of investments or loaded into one or two kinds?

What happens if you leave? Can you take the money with you or must you leave it in the company's fund?

And what protection is there if the company goes bankrupt? While future benefits can't be insured, are the contributions protected so you can get money out if things go wrong?

Those are things you need to know about your retirement plan.

Defined Benefit Plans

Defined benefit plans are great for people who stay with companies a long time. Most will increase with inflation. All are federally insured for benefits up to $21,600 in 1988.

Sounds good, doesn't it? But not knowing how these plans work can leave you with a false assumption about what you'll get when you retire.

One common characteristic of such plans is that they are calculated based upon your legal retirement date. How they are calculated can make a big difference to you.

There are two basic formulas for determining your benefit.

Flat Dollar. No, this doesn't mean that you'll get freshly pressed money when you retire. It means you'll get a specific dollar amount each year after you retire. For example, you might get $15 a month for each year of service. For 25 years, your monthly benefit would be $375 or $4,500 a year. Note: The more years you work the bigger your pension which is true with all pension plans.

Flat-dollar pensions are most commonly negotiated through labor unions, which look out for their retired members by seeking inflation protection for benefits and help current workers by seeking to increase benefits in future years by tying them to increases in wages or trading wage increases for better retirement benefits.

If you are a member of a union that has negotiated a pension for you, contact your benefits officer to review how your plan works. Focus on what inflation protection you can expect and what percentage of your current wages your pension and Social Security will replace.

If you can't expect any inflation protection, you're stuck with a fixed income. That means you'll have to have more savings when you retire and must plan to save more after you retire. You don't want to see your standard of living gradually decline. The fact that you're growing older doesn't mean you have to let inflation compound your problems and leave you flat.

Percentage of Salary. This means exactly what it says. Your pension will be a percentage of your salary. But what your "salary" is to which the percentage is applied can be the difference between your retirement being a thick piece of cake and it being a thin slice for life.

Take career average formulas. *Please*. Who wants to be average? Yet, there are two types of such formulas.

Under one type, you earn a little piece of your pay as it is recognized for the purpose of the retirement plan for each year you work. Your benefit then will equal the sum of all those itty-bitty pieces earned each year. You just hope they add up to something you can live on when you retire.

The second type of career average formula totals up your pay during your participation in the plan. Your benefit will equal a percentage of your career average pay multiplied by the number of years of service. Thus, your high earning later years will be averaged with your low earning early years. And you get caught in the middle—that is at a much lower standard of living than the years before you retire. That's why you'll want to save like mad after you rise above average.

This mediocre pension plan has been made a little better by some employers. They put in a breakpoint, after which a higher percentage of your earnings in your later years of employment is applied to your pension benefit formula than for your early years of employment. That's a big break for you, but not as good as a final-earnings formula.

Your biggest retirement break is provided by what are called final-pay formulas. It sounds rather grim, but it isn't. Basically, a final-pay plan bases your benefits on your average earnings over your last three to five years with your company. As with other defined benefit plans, it will take into account your years of service. The longer you work with a company, the bigger your benefit. And with a formula that pays you that benefit based upon your highest earning years, that's the best protection you could have for inflation.

To highlight the difference between a final-pay plan and an average-pay plan, consider Mary Contrary and Joe E. Day.

Joe E. Day worked 35 years as a Pelican feeder for the Birds, an aviary by the sea. When he started as a bait cutter he earned $75 a week. This gradually increased to $90 a week and after five years, Joe E. earned a promotion to fish catcher. He then earned $130 a week, which rose to $250 before his promotion to fish inspector after twelve years. Then he began a meteoric climb—to chief fish inspector, to manager of slop and catch, to division chief for inspection of fish, to chief of pelican operations.

In his final year before retirement, Joe E. was earning $1,650 a week. His annual income had climbed from $3,900 when he started, and an average of $4,342 a year for his first five years, to $6,760 a year, and an average of $9,980 for his next 12 years, to $85,800 a year when he retired, and an average of $75,240 over his last five years. Over his entire 35 years, his average pay was $27,800. And his pension, well, this everyday Joe had an average-pay formula. So, his pension was pegged to his average pay over his career—$13,900 a year. Considering that prices went up 250 percent over his career, that meant his pension was worse than his pay when he fished or cut bait.

Mary Contrary, on the other hand, began in the secretarial pool of Hi-Rise Development. She was back in the stacks for 20 years, her pay increasing during that span from $37.50 a week to $190 a week. But night classes and a civil rights discrimination complaint which ended her employer's discriminatory promotion practices that led to her promotion out of the secretarial pool to administrative assistant to the treasurer, then head of administrative services, and finally chief of development support services. The year before she retired, she earned $1,122 a week—68 percent of what Joe E. Day made his last year. Her last five years she earned only 66 percent as much on average as Joe—$49,658 a year. Her career average salary was only 62 percent of Joe's—$17,236. But her pension was based on her last five years, so her pension was $24,829—79 percent more than Joe's.

The moral? Career-average earning pensions are for the birds.

But notice, too, that even with final-average formulas, you don't pick up 50 percent of your last year's pay. Mary Contrary still only earned 43 percent of her final year's pay. Even with a maximum Social Security payment, she would earn only about 62 percent of her final year's pay. So, she still needed to save.

Her problem (and yours) may be that your company might not simply provide you a pension, it may "integrate" your pension with Social Security benefits—reducing your combined pension and Social Security benefits.

"Integration" sounds like social policy. It means to put together. But in pensions, integration can tear your retirement apart.

One form of integration in pensions is to set up a benefit goal for your retirement, usually at a percentage of your pre-retirement income. Your pension is only what is needed to reach that percentage of your income. Another form is the offset plan. It reduces your pension by a certain percentage of your Social Security benefits.

Such offsets and goals primarily work to the benefit of higher-wage workers and the detriment of low- and middle-income workers.

Take a $200,000-a-year executive and a middle manager earning $48,300, the current maximum wage on which Social Security taxes are levied on you and your employer. Let's say those were the average salaries for the last five years, each employee worked at least 25 years with the company, and the employer is using a final-average formula.

The executive and the middle manager will get a maximum of $11,800 in Social Security—$5,900 of which were employee-paid by their contributions and $5,900 of which the employer can claim. At a goal of 50 percent for the retirement plan, the executive would get a pension of $100,000 and the middle manager would get $24,150. But for the executive, the company would pay 94 percent of the benefit—$100,000 – $5,900 = $94,100, which is 94 percent. For the middle manager, the company would pay only 76 percent of the benefit—$18,250.

For lower income workers, the differential is even more because Social Security replaces more income at lower levels.

Integration is Social Security for the rich.

You can be thankful about a couple of things. Uncle Sam has limited the maximum amount that an employer can offset. The government has set a minimum level of compensation for lower-level personnel. That minimum is 2 percent of pay for year of service, up to 20 percent of pay.

Still, if your company says it will replace up to 50 percent of your income when you retire, make sure you understand how they are going to replace it.

- Will your pension be integrated with Social Security, and how will it be integrated?

- Will your pension be based upon your average wage or an average of so many years at the end of your employment?

- Will you suffer any loss in pension rights or vesting for a break in service?

- Will your pension be based upon all your compensation or only your base pay or only your pay above a certain level? Employers have tremendous discretion in that area.

- Will your pension increase with inflation or be fixed the minute you retire?

- What will your pension be if you quit right now and move to another job, or if you are fired?

   You need to know these things now so you can plan for your retirement and so you can fill in the blanks of the retirement savings form (Worksheet 5.1) at the beginning of this Chapter with some reasonable expectation your projections will be true.

   Once you're sure of them, you'll know what you'll need to save. And beginning in the next Chapter, that's what you'll learn how to start doing better.

6

Before You Invest: Saving that Cold, Hard Cash

One of the simplest equations in economics is I = S, investment = savings. It doesn't exactly mean what it looks like it means. Investment doesn't always equal savings. Often, it is less than savings. During the Great Depression, it was usually much less than savings, unless you counted as an investment in bedding the money people saved by hiding it away under their mattresses.

Just think of Ollie North. He had a $15,000 savings pool that he kept in a box in his home—just for emergencies. You couldn't exactly say that was an investment. You also couldn't exactly say that was very smart. If it was stolen from his home, he could never get it back. If his house burned down, it would have gone up in smoke. Saving that old-fashioned way was stupid. Not that North was stupid, but the action was. History will have to judge North now that the courts have had their say. Just don't let your money lie idly about as he did his.

But what the equation I = S really tells you is that your investment can't be any greater than your savings. And before you invest, you must save.

That's true even for those who borrow to invest. Borrowers must put up collateral for those loans, unless they have a kindly, rich aunt, or, in the case of savings and loan associations, a deficit-ridden old uncle willing to guarantee the loans if they don't meet their obligations to lenders—the people with deposits in S&Ls.

CONTROLLING YOUR SPENDING

The first step you must make before you invest, though, is to save. And now we go back to your budget.

In Chapter 1 I suggested some "quick-save" ideas to help you achieve some savings, to cut your grocery bill, for example. This Chapter deals with a method to achieve further savings by working through your budget and looking at your future income.

Most people spend as if they were on autopilot, only worse. A plane on autopilot at least has a direction; even if it can't land, it will fly in that direction until it runs out of gas and crashes. People often don't even have a direction. They never establish a goal for their spending and thus can't have a goal for saving either. They just continue on their merry way until they run out of gas and crash—usually at retirement time.

The whole purpose of the budget, the little spending book you've been carrying around, and your net worth statement is to point out that you can control your spending. You make choices now, of course. But you tend to make them unconsciously. You get by with whatever you have on hand—whatever it is. You've been, as a friend of mine likes to tell me at times, "like a Zombie." You need to get some direction.

The goal you set in the last Chapter provided you some direction. You know what you need to save and ultimately invest if you are to retire comfortably. But you may not know exactly how to get your retirement plan off the ground.

Think. Think of how you spend. Look at your budget and see how you spend. Most likely, you fill the space available—you spend what you've got.

That's what you've got to stop doing. How?

Simple. Divide your budget into percentages.

What percentage of your income do you spend on rent or mortgage payments? Is it 20 percent? 30 percent? What percentage do you spend on your car payments? 5 percent? 10 percent? What have you allocated for furniture? Clothing? Percentage it all out.

Now take a look at each item. How many of them will increase? Do you think they'll all increase at the rate of inflation? Not likely. Some of those items will remain fixed. Even if you rent, usually the amount is fixed for at least 12 months. Car payments are fixed for the term of your loan. Make use of those facts to generate savings, because more than likely your income will increase, either with or a little faster than inflation. And as it does, you won't have to spend as much of it for them.

That should make you happy. But don't do what most people do—get a raise and just spend whatever they've got. Rather than enjoy a gradual rise in their living standard they try to leap ahead. Consequently they fall behind in savings and don't have much money to invest.

To generate savings, think of all your expense items as increasing right along with your income. Then allocate budget money for each of them accordingly. Every month when it comes time to pay the bills, take the money you don't need for those items and put it into your retirement account. That's called paying yourself *first*.

The key is to do it for *all* your expenses. Not just a few. That way anything that increases less than your income will generate savings; those items that increase as fast as your income will be taken care of. This way you'll be in control, and you won't feel like you're being squeezed all the time.

Let me show you how it works on a monthly level.

Easy Mark was making $3,200 a month, then he got a raise to $3,500 a month. His percentage budget before and after his raise looked like that shown in Table 6.1.

Even without tightening his belt on items like groceries, entertainment, or his vacation, Mark was able to put aside an *extra* $109.80 for savings for a total of $142.80—simply by budgeting his income by percentages, which in his case would amount to more than $1,300 a year in *additional* savings. The only real effort was Mark's being aware of what he was spending and then putting some of it aside.

TABLE 6.1 Monthly Percentage Budget for Easy Mark

Exp. Item	% Exp., $3,200/mo.	% of Income	% Exp., $3,500/mo.	Act. Exp., $3,500/mo.	Savings, $3,500/mo.
Mortgage	$800.00	25.00%	$875.00	$800.00	$75.00
Utilities	200.00	6.25	218.75	201.00	17.25
Property tax	100.00	3.13	109.55	100.00	9.55
(calculated at $1,200 ÷ 12)					
Income tax	480.00	15.00	525.00	540.00	(15.00)
Social Security	240.00	7.50	262.50	262.50	—
Telephone	50.00	1.57	55.00	50.00	5.00
Car payment	250.00	7.81	273.00	250.00	23.00
Groceries	300.00	9.38	328.00	333.00	(5.00)
Vacations	200.00	6.25	218.75	218.75	—
(two week cruise)					
Personal care	50.00	1.57	55.00	55.00	—
Entertainment	400.00	12.50	437.50	435.00	2.50
Other	100.00	3.12	109.00	112.00	(3.00)
Savings	30.00	0.94	**33.00**	**142.80**	**109.80**
Total	$3,200.00	100.00%	$3,500.00	$3,500.00	

Of course, it won't be quite that much because inflation will eat into some—but not all—of it. About $84 comes from savings on fixed-cost items (mortgage and car payment). That savings won't just disappear, unless Mark allows it to.

As future raises occur and as long as Mark continues to percentage his budget, he will be able to increase savings each year through this allocation formula.

For example, the following year Mark got another $300-a-month-raise. Again, he allocated 25 percent for his mortgage, 7.81 percent for his car payment, right on through to his savings. Because his expenses for most of those items didn't increase as much as his income, he was able to put another $120 of that increase into savings, which increased his monthly savings to $262.75.

An emergency at the end of the year resulted in a $500 payout, but by the end of the year he still had more than $3,600 in savings—$1,000 from the first year, $2,500 from the second year, and more than $100 in interest generated by his savings invested in certificates of deposit.

The third year, his savings increased to $3,600, bringing his total to $7,500, including $300 in interest. The fourth year, he had $4,800, for a total of $13,050, including $750 in interest. And in five years, he had $20,300, including $1,250 in interest.

Incredible? Hardly. All this kind of savings plan does is take advantage of income growth and the likelihood that at least some of your cost items will increase less than your income. Most, in fact, because your income is likely to increase a little faster than inflation while the market basket of goods you buy increases only with inflation.

It also takes advantage of compounding. Savings, like interest, compound. Each year's savings can be built into the budget so that it will increase even more the next year. And even more the next year after that. And so on.

But because this kind of savings plan allocates more for entertainment and vacations, you will enjoy your increased income. You'll have a higher living standard and you won't feel like you're just running in place. Instead, you'll be in control because you are following a plan.

All it takes is a little discipline to work through the budget, divide it into percentages, and then allocate by those percentages with each successive raise.

The money for vacations goes up. The money for entertainment goes up. The money for groceries and utilities and telephone conversations goes up. Your living standard increases. But you save—by a plan. And your savings increase each year.

PLANNING SAVES MONEY

Of course, you can save even more. Mark was lazy: He didn't cut any of his spending. He didn't do anything except stay awake enough to percentage out his budget and then allocate money by his increases in pay.

Looking through your budget and at your budget book, you should be wide awake enough to stop wasting money.

One of the biggest areas of waste in most family budgets is food. I told you in Chapter 1 that just a 5 percent savings in a weekly food budget of $100 would amount to $260 a year. But most people can do even better than that.

How? By watching how your family eats and by planning meals.

For example, if you buy soda pop, get screw-top bottles instead of cans. Why? Because with a can, you feel you have to drink it all. It's just like people who spend without a budget. It's there, so you use it. If you have to pour pop into a glass, you'll have pop left over, not drink as much, lose weight, feel better—and save money.

The same is true for potato chips. An uncle of mine used to have a big tin can with a lid. Every time he bought chips, he'd put them in the can to keep them fresh. He'd serve the chips themselves from a bowl. If he'd left the bag out, I would have eaten the whole bag, but I was just as satisfied eating less from a bowl. From him, I found out that while you may not be able to eat just one, you don't have to eat them all.

You can probably think of other strategies.

Just remember: Budgeting your expenses is no different than creating a menu. And creating a menu for eating is budgeting your food dollars. So, if you don't want them to go to waste don't let the food you eat go to waist—thoughtlessly.

Create a menu—of snacks and of meals. And plan it through thoroughly. For example, think in a cycle. Start your week with a major meal—a roast, chicken, or something else that offers leftovers. Follow that with meals that complement the meat of your major meal. Then finish the week by using the rest of the leftovers and the meat to make soup.

If you have a pork roast, make pork chop suey—that's really what chop suey is supposed to be—leftovers.

If you have spaghetti, use the sauce as a base for chili or another meal.

Ham? Bean soup. Pot roast? Stew.

And intersperse them with some simple meals—waffles or pancakes with tuna salad—foods that won't eat up your budget yet still provide varied sources of protein, vitamins, and minerals.

Well-planned menus will cut down on shopping time and time spent in the kitchen. They'll also save you money—up to $20 a week for most families.

The half hour or so you spend weekly on menu planning is a lot less time than you'll waste every day if you have to think about what to have for dinner.

So start menu-planning along with your budgeting. And if you have trouble, I'll send you some recipes.

Use the same approach to planning vacations. Each month Mark put money aside for his vacation, and it was a big one. A cruise.

Thinking about what you want to do for a vacation provides a goal and something to look forward to.

It also can provide extra savings.

How?

If you plan a vacation, you can get a travel agent who can tell you what trips are available, when the high and low seasons are, when you might enjoy going, and how to spend less money.

Of course, you don't want to visit Florida in July or Nova Scotia in January. That may be super cheap, but it also can be super miserable because of the weather.

Go for the "shoulder" seasons that fall in between. Rates are cheaper, usually the weather is good, and such trips can save money.

You can anticipate the cost of your trip and thus put money aside. Mark's $2,400 vacation didn't just "happen." Each month he put aside $200—the first three donations into a nine-month certificate of deposit that earned 9 percent, the next three into six-month certificates that earned 8.25 percent, the next three into three-month certificates that earned 7.5 percent, and the last into one-month rollovers that earned 6.75 percent.

He earned almost $100 in interest doing that. Not a lot. But if you do it for two or three vacations, it, too, can add up.

Planning saves money. That's what using your budget should help you do. Whatever you have to save for, budget, put the money into something that earns interest, and then you'll generate income for savings. You'll turn your expenses into instruments of savings—and investment.

Which is what the next Chapter is about.

7

Investment Basics: It's a Risky Business

No pain, no gain. Why does everything you want to get require some sacrifice? If you want high returns on your investments, you have to sacrifice some security. If you want security, you have to sacrifice some high returns. So much for the idea that you can have it all.

But you can have good thick slices of both. You can, with a little effort and figuring, get higher returns without sacrificing too much security. As long as you understand the risks and have a goal for your investments.

Going back to Chapter 6 and the amount you need to save for retirement, you know that the more your investments earn, the less you have to save to reach your retirement goal.

How much less? Take a $1,000 investment. In Table 7.1 you'll see the differences in what you would earn at different interest rates over time if you compounded your gains annually.

TABLE 7.1 Earnings at Varying Interest Rates and Periods on a $1,000 Investment

Years	Interest Rates									
	1%	2%	3%	4%	5%	6%	7%	8%	9%	10%
5	$51	$104	$159	$217	$276	$338	$402	$469	$539	$611
10	105	218	355	480	628	791	967	1158	1367	1594
15	161	346	558	801	1078	1396	1759	2172	2642	3177
20	220	486	806	1191	1653	2207	2870	3661	4604	5727

Of course, interest rates don't occur in a vacuum. Inflation pumps up interest rates and deflates the return of any investment. For example, a 7 percent inflation rate decreases the purchasing power of your $1,000 investment each year. If you just held $1,000 in a drawer for 20 years, you'd be able to buy only about 25.8 percent as much when you took it out as when you put it in the drawer—it would have a real value of only $258. So, if you earned 10 percent compounded annually on an investment over 20 years, the $5,727 you earned plus your initial $1,000 investment would have a real value of $1,738 if inflation averaged 7 percent.

Still, that's a heck of a lot better than the "real" $1,204 your investment would be worth at 8 percent compounded annually. At 1 percentage point above inflation, you would have to commit 1.44 times as much to savings over 20 years or save for an additional nine years than if you earned 3 points more than the inflation rate.

To get a higher return, you have to accept some more risk. That means you can't afford to be a totally passive investor. You can't just leave your money in certificates of deposit or a savings account and expect to accumulate enough to meet your retirement income goals. But to accept more risk, you have to know what the risks are.

WHAT ARE THE RISKS OF INVESTMENTS?

There are three types of investment risks.

First, there are personal risks. Is your job secure and that of your spouse, if both of you work? If they aren't, you'll need to be ready to ride out the bumps and should have more short-term assets—such as money market accounts or stocks or other securities you can sell quickly. Do you have young children? You will need to put more aside for their education and will need to buy more life insurance to provide them financial protection in case of your death.

Second, there are the risks inherent with investing in any particular company, piece of property, or commodity. A company can go bankrupt due to bad management. Property may be located in an area that isn't growing in population or adding new businesses. A commodity may cease to be scarce and go down in price.

To defray risk of owning a particular asset, you need to buy a variety of stocks, or bonds, or pieces of real estate, or different commodities, or buy certificates of deposit at a variety of banks, or buy numerous Treasury issues. If you're rich, you can cover every contingency. But if you were rich, would you be worried about retirement?

So, because you aren't rich, you have to buy at least some investments that diversify your holdings automatically, such as mutual funds, real estate investment trusts (REITs), commodity funds, or money market funds.

But if you invest only in mutual funds, or only in REITs, or only in commodity funds, or put all your money into CDs at different banks, you'll protect yourself against the risks of owning a particular asset but not against the third category of risk—marketplace and general economic risk.

If you put all your money into stocks or mutual funds and inflation galloped ahead as it did in the 1970s, your investments might drop in real value. Stocks tend to perform best when inflation rates are below 4 percent, for understandable reasons. Just as inflation eats into your pay during the year, it also costs companies more to do business. Their borrowing costs go up. Their workers demand more pay. They may not be able to sell as many goods if consumers feel their pocketbooks being pinched by higher prices.

Those things cut profits, dividends, and stock prices. They reduce funds for research and development of new products—and that cuts the company's potential for growth and its stock prices even more.

Bonds are affected similarly. New investors demand more for their investments—higher interest rates—so the prices of existing bonds fall. While that won't reduce your return from a bond, you can't sell it for as much as you bought it for. That can make you feel poorer because, in fact, you are.

Meanwhile, other investments, such as money market funds, short-term certificates of deposit, many kinds of investment real estate, and certain commodities, such as gold, usually increase in value as inflation rises.

But if you have to sell off all of your assets to get in on that parade, what happens? Inflation may abate. Stock prices will go up again, bond prices will rise, too, as interest rates go down. And then when you try to catch up to that investment parade, you'll come in buying fewer shares than before because you sold low and will have to buy back in as prices for those investments rise.

Different economic conditions affect different kinds of investment in different ways.

If inflation is rising or at a high level and the economy is slowing down or has gone into a recession, you want cash in money markets or short-term CDs. The worst investments to be holding are long-term bonds. Their prices would have to fall so the interest they earn can match those on new CDs, money market accounts, and bond issues.

If inflation is falling and economic growth is slowing, holding cash in a money market is a bad investment. Long-term bonds are the best investment to be holding. But if the economy is growing fast and inflation is falling or steady, you'll be in great shape if you hold stocks.

Gold does great in inflationary times and lousy when prices are holding steady. In fact, its value was cut in half during the 1980s. Real estate does well when the economy is growing and prices are rising, not so well when prices are rising and the economy is slowing, worse still if inflation is falling and the economy is growing, and worst of all when inflation is falling and there's a recession.

How do you handle all these different risks without feeling you've been put through a mixmaster? How do you protect your retirement from the risk of losing it all? There's no magic formula. Just use your common sense and don't panic.

Investors did panic during the October 1987 Stock Market Crash—even professional money managers and some managers of mutual funds got caught in the selling craze. Afterward, those investors who held on did a lot better than those that followed the bellowing of the bears. The stock market rebounded—not all at once—but over a period of two years. And the bad news bears missed the honey pot.

Does this mean you should just buy and hold onto investments forever? That strategy isn't the worst in the world. Over time, most investments will pan out, as long as they are based on fundamentally sound investment principles—the same principles I will soon outline for picking a good stock to invest in.

You should avoid investments sold with gimmicks, such as being a super tax break. Limited partnerships have had a rocky road since the Tax Reform Act (TRA) of 1986. They've had to switch from investments that provide tax deductions to assets that actually make money the old fashioned way—serving a real consumer need.

TAX DEDUCTIONS AND TRA 1986

What tax reform did was divide losses from investments into four types: business losses, capital losses, investment losses, and passive losses.

Business losses are those from a business you are actually engaged in. They are fully deductible from any income you have—salary, dividends, interest, rents. One primary kind of business activity many people take on is that of landlord. They become owner of a house or duplex and rent it out. If you make less than $150,000 a year, you can deduct the losses from that enterprise as an active business loss.

The key thing about a business loss is that it has to be a real business, and to show that it is, you must make money every three out of five years. Otherwise the IRS will classify your business as a hobby. And you can't deduct your expenses for a hobby. The rule makes sense because otherwise would-be stamp, coin, and art collectors who do it for pleasure would stick Uncle Sam with part of the cost of their fun.

Capital losses are losses from the sale of investments—if you sell an investment for less than you paid for it. You can deduct capital losses from gains you've made in the sale of investments. But you can only deduct $3,000 a year in such losses from salary, interest, and dividend income. If your losses exceed your gains by more than $3,000, you can deduct that loss from your gains the next year and up to $3,000 from your income. And you can keep doing that until the total loss is deducted.

The key to capital losses is that you can deduct a loss only from an investment. If you sell your home for less than you bought it, you can't deduct that loss. The same thing for a couch or a television set. If you sell a piece of art and lose money on the sale, you'll have to prove to the IRS that it was bought as an investment. Again, the reason for the rule is simple. We buy a lot of stuff just to enjoy or because we need it. We aren't buying those things expecting them to increase in value. We know that for the most part they won't. And we've used them. And the government isn't there to help us pay for what we use, just as it shouldn't tax us for income we didn't make.

Investment losses basically are interest payments on loans a person may have taken out to make an investment. Just as a business can deduct from its profits the interest paid on loans to buy equipment or land or material, so an individual can deduct the interest paid to purchase investments from the profits he or she makes investing. Under the old rules, that interest was also deductible from ordinary income. Tax reform has phased out the deduction from ordinary income, but you can still deduct it from interest, dividends, royalties, and net capital gains (the gain after deducting capital losses).

Passive losses are generated by what used to be a big industry in this country, the tax-shelter industry, including limited partnerships. Passive losses— like depreciation—were passed through to investors to deduct against their income. Tax reform is phasing out the deducting of passive losses against ordinary income. By 1991, it will be limited to deductions against passive income, which basically amounts to rental income from a limited partnership.

If you have income or losses generated by limited partnerships or other tax shelters, talk to a tax expert. The area is so confusing that even the IRS has been unable to give satisfactory answers.

The tax consequences of investments can't be ignored. Not when federal and state taxes can eat up to 40 percent of your investment earnings. There are ways to lessen that bite, as I will go into later. But the risk of taxes to your retirement nest egg only makes it more important for you to look for businesses, limited partnerships, REITs, and mutual funds that have managers with a good track record and with goals of making products or providing services people need or want. Only those firms will make enough profit over time to allow your investments to grow after you buy them.

But how do you find those firms? How do you shoulder all the risks of investing? How do you keep from missing opportunities and opening yourself to greater risk? Well, one way is to go to experts for help—financial planners and brokers.

BROKERS, PLANNERS, AND OTHER CREATURE FEATURES

A bad investment advisor is the biggest risk to your financial well being. Highwaymen were at least up front about what they did: "Your money or your life." Bad investment counselors, planners, brokers will tell you how they are out to make you money and then ruin your investment life.

There are good ones out there. Although you wouldn't think so from recent polls. Two-thirds of Americans say their financial advisors put their own self-interest before that of the client, according to a *Money*/ABC News Poll. (For a quick rundown on finding financial advice you can trust, see the November 1989 issue of *Money*, pp. 80-96. A more complete analysis of how to deal with a stock broker can be found in Anne Grant's *Keeping Your Stock Broker Honest*, published by IPC, 625 N. Michigan Ave., Chicago, IL 60611).

What makes it so tough is that most financial advisors have a built-in conflict of interest. Stock brokers are interested mostly in you buying and selling because they make money on the trades, not on whether or not you make money. Financial planners receive incentives from firms selling investments.

So how can you find a financial advisor you can trust?

First, you have to decide what kind of advice you want and what you can afford.

If you are basically going to deal in blue chip stocks and bonds, mutual funds and real estate investment trusts (REITs), you can do most of your own evaluations, and this book will give an idea of how to do so.

For making those kinds of investments, you can either buy directly from the firms offering them, work through your bank, or go to a discount broker to place your order. Discount brokers' services are cheaper than the fees and commissions charged by full-service brokers—from 50 percent to 80 percent less.

If you want to get involved with limited partnerships, highly speculative stocks and bonds, and new companies, you need a full-service broker. Primarily, so you will have someone to scream at if you lose all your hard earned dough.

Just kidding. Sort of.

Really, if you plan to be an active trader in speculative ventures, you'll need a good broker whose interest in making money off you will encourage him or her to provide some direction to your entrepreneurial spirit.

To find that good broker, or a good discount broker if you plan to make your own brilliant choices and dumb mistakes, you must shop around. Ask friends if they like their brokers. If they do, then ask them why. If it's because they make a good golf partner, that might not be what you need. You aren't looking for a buddy but someone who will give you sound investment advice.

That means knowing why you are investing—what your objectives are and what you're going to use the broker for.

To get a foot in the door, what you might do is check into brokerage individual retirement accounts (IRAs). By asking what's available in those, you have an immediate objective—something to talk to people at the brokerage firm about. And in doing that, you can find out what fees and commissions they charge to handle IRAs and other accounts.

Go to three or four brokerage houses and check into IRAs—that's an order.

If you find you like one after visiting all four, check with your state securities commission and contact the Freedom of Information Office of the Securities and Exchange Commission, 450 Fifth St. N.W., Mail Stop 2-6, Washington, D.C. 20549, for past disciplinary actions and complaints about the broker. Brokers are regulated by the SEC and should be registered with the National Association of Securities Dealers. But that doesn't mean they have a spotless background. Check it out. Then, if the broker you like checks out, open an IRA and branch out from that. More wading, more knowledge, more investing.

If a broker tries to take over your investment decisions, fails to offer alternatives, or keeps suggesting investments that don't pan out, get another. Remember the bottom line is that they like you for the commissions you generate; you like them for the advice and services they provide. If you don't provide them commissions by buying and selling, they won't like you. If they don't provide good service and advice, you don't have to like them. Simple.

Never feel intimidated by a broker. Never invest in something you don't understand. Never pretend to understand something you don't, no matter how tempting that is. And never lie to them about why you've decided to do something. If you don't feel comfortable with an investment they suggest, tell them so. Never let them suck you in with lines like, "Well, I've come to you three times, don't you trust me?" or "This is really hot." If you don't understand it or feel comfortable about it, don't invest. It's your money, not theirs.

The primary reason you may need a full-service broker is for information. Brokerages have research departments that should be able to fill in the details on investments you consider. You should be able to ask them about the research department. Don't expect, though, to use the broker like a library. If you waste a broker's time in meaningless searches for information when you really don't plan to invest, they won't like it. When you ask for information, you should be planning to make an investment. The information they give you will tell whether the investment you're considering is a good one or if there is a better one in the category—stocks, bonds, or commodity funds—that you were thinking of putting money into.

If your broker leaves his or her nest, you may not want to follow if the research provided by the brokerage house was good. On his or her own, or with another firm, research may not be as good.

So, here is the basic rundown on getting and dealing with a broker:

1. Seek the lowest fees you can for the services you want. If you're going to invest primarily in mutual funds and CDs, do it directly. They're easy to research, and you shouldn't waste your investment money on fees and commissions.

2. Set your goals before deciding what you'll invest in—including the level of risk you're willing to take to achieve bigger gains.

3. Invest only in things you understand.

4. Keep your relationship with your stock broker on a business-like level. If you think making a broker your friend will get you a better deal, forget it. That isn't how it works.

5. Always ask for alternatives to the specific investment a broker suggests, what the broker will get out of the investment suggested, and why that is better than the alternatives.

6. Never, never, never hand over to a broker control of your account to make investments without your approval. That is the equivalent of investment suicide.

Keeping those things in mind, a stock broker can help put your money to work for you.

Dealing with a financial planner is more difficult. The financial planning industry is almost totally unregulated unless the planner happens to be an insurance agent or a broker, and certification of planners means next to nothing unless the planner is a certified public accountant.

Again, you may have to count upon friends to help find a good financial planner. But only hire one that works for a fee, not a commission. And use them primarily to set up a plan for diversification, not to buy and sell securities for you. Never give them discretion over your bank account. And if you use them for specific investment advice, always ask for alternative investments. And expressly ask if they get bonuses, trips, or other incentives for any security you might buy through them.

If your portfolio of investments is worth less than $100,000, don't expect a lot of attention from either a stock broker or a financial planner. You simply don't have enough money to churn commissions or fees. They want $2,000 a year from a customer, which means at least $25,000 a year in investment activity. And if the investments they put you in are so bad that you have to turn them over every four years, how good can they really be? That inattention, though, may be a blessing, as sometimes the wisest counsel is one's own, if you develop a solid investment strategy, a topic we'll discuss in the next Chapter.

8

Safe Investments, or Buy Low, Sell High

So, you've got some money put aside. Now what? You look at a stock chart and it's confusing. Companies can default on bonds. Real estate is tricky, look what's happening to the savings and loans. Art? I can't tell a Renoir from a Rennie Orr.

So many different kinds of investments. "Maybe," you think, "I'll just leave my money in the bank."

The bank is a good place to start. But not in a simple savings account.

Newcomers to investing need to get their feet wet. But not in anything risky. Not until they learn some of the language of the marketplace, find reliable brokers or money managers, and make informed investment decisions.

You can't just hand your savings over to somebody else and hope they'll make you rich. It's your money, and you have to be the boss on how it's handled. So you have to do some swimming in the investment pool.

This Chapter will give you a rundown of some of the different types of investments you can make—primarily the so-called safe investments. We'll then look at so-called growth investments that entail more risk and more reward. Then we'll go into the mixing and matching, using as a model the 401(K) plan or the IRA to provide some tax shelters for your income while you save for retirement.

But first, let's go to the bank.

CERTIFICATES OF DEPOSIT

One of the things you see outside of every bank door is a list of interest rates tied to different times. You see figures of 30, 60, 90 days, all the way up to five years.

Usually the longer the period, the higher the interest.

These savings vehicles are called Certificates of deposit (CDs). They are available to anyone who has enough money to put down. And "enough" can range from $100 to $5,000. Most often, the minimum is $1,000. Certificates of Deposit can make you money. And at little risk.

Risks with CDs are very low because they are federally insured up to $100,000 at most banks and credit unions. Just be careful not to confuse them with certain kinds of uninsured bonds that financial institutions sell, usually at higher interest rates.

The important thing about CDs for your purposes is that they yield more interest than a savings account and are a good place to put your money while you learn about other kinds of investments.

That doesn't mean that you should simply plop all your money into a five-year CD while you think about it, although you could have done worse over the past five years.

A five-year $1,000 CD bought in 1983 when they were first marketed earned the holder $850 by the time it was sold. That's a pretty good return, considering inflation was only about 20 percent for that entire period—or $200.

But it still wouldn't have matched the return for stocks, even after the October 1987 stock market crash. They went up 100 percent—$1,000—in the same five-year period.

And interest rates in 1983 were exceedingly high following our bout with inflation in the late 1970s and early 1980s. In fact, that five-year CD paid 13 percent interest.

If you see many of those, it would be worth plugging your money into— quick. But that's not likely unless inflation goes sky high.

In that event, what you want to do is have money to invest at the highest interest rates you can get.

How do you do that? Simple. You *don't* put all your savings into one CD, you put it into CDs of varying maturities.

Sure, that means a little work and a little lower interest rate. But remember: Your goal is to earn some extra money with your CDs while you continue to learn how to make even more. And you take advantage of fluctuating interest rates to earn a good average annual return.

Here's what you do. Say your retirement nest egg is $5,000. Take $1,000 and put it into a 180-day CD, put another $1,000 into a 90-day CD, and put another $2,000 into a 60-day CD, and, finally, put $1,000 into a 30-day CD.

When the 30-day CD matures, put $1,000 into a six-month CD.

When the 60-day CD matures, put $1,000 into a 90-day CD and $1,000 into a 180-day CD.

When the next 90-day CD matures, put that into a 30-day CD, which you then roll over into a 180-day CD when it matures.

And when the 90-day CD in which you invested with your 60-day CD matures, you put that into a 180-day CD.

Sound confusing? Look at Table 8.1.

TABLE 8.1 Investing in CDs of Varying Maturities or Getting the Highest Interest From CDs

CD Maturity	Investment Strategy					
	Start	30 Days	60 Days	90 Days	120 Days	180 Days
30	$1,000	x	x	$1,000	x	x
60	2,000	2,000	x	x	x	x
90	1,000	1,000	2,000	1,000	1,000	x
180	1,000	2,000	3,000	4,000	5,000	6,000

The objective is to get all your money into 180-day CDs where they'll have the best return, but also leave you within reach of $1,000 for either emergencies or to make other investments.

Eventually you'll want to move your money out of CDs into other kinds of investments. Until you decide, you'll want to earn the most interest at the least risk and greatest liquidity—and this method of getting into 180-day CDs is a good way to do that.

There are other simple accounts where you can invest your savings. All have advantages and disadvantages. Here are some of them.

MONEY MARKET ACCOUNTS

Like CDs, money market accounts are quick, easy investments to make. And they are as available as the nearest bank.

The only problem is the interest on money market accounts tends to be lower than that for CDs—at least historically. During that 1983-88 period, for example, money markets earned less than $450 for a $1,000 investment. And you have to keep a minimum of $1,000 in them. Money markets are a good place to park cash that you're about ready to invest, though. If you have enough, you can use it like a checking account and get decent interest without any risk, as such accounts are federally insured.

But to make any real money with money market accounts, you have to invest in money market mutual funds that are themselves invested in Treasury bills, short-term CDs, and corporate debt. Such accounts are handled by brokerage houses. What you get with such a fund is management expertise. If you decide on a money market mutual fund, remember that not all managers are equal, and therefore all funds won't provide an equally good return.

U.S. SAVINGS BONDS

These are about the lowest-risk investment you can make. They aren't just *insured* by the federal government, they literally *are* the federal government—savings bonds finance the nation's $3 trillion debt. You can get them through payroll deductions or at your bank or credit union.

Savings bonds are very cheap—$25 for a minimum Series EE bond that has a face value of $50 when it matures in 10 years.

The greatest advantage of savings bonds is that they defer taxes on the interest you earn. And when rates for bonds are within a percentage point of the returns offered by other types of interest-bearing investments, they can make sense.

Compare the return of a $1,000 tax-deferred savings bond over 10 years earning 7.5 percent versus a series of 180-day CDs earning an average of 8.25 percent over the same 10-year period. The savings bond will be worth $2,060 at maturity. Even if you pay taxes on the $1,060 in earnings at a 28 percent rate at the time of maturity, you'll have made $770. That's almost equal to an actual 5.9 percent annual rate of return compounded over the 10-year period.

The CDs, in the meantime, even with your constantly reinvesting them and investing the interest, will garner you an actual rate of return of just slightly more than 6 percent after taxes; that's hardly worth the effort.

But if the difference is anything more than a percentage point, compounding and reinvesting will earn you much more, even after taxes, than a savings bond.

Having the money in CDs gives you flexibility you don't have with savings bonds. The five to ten years you must have your money invested in a savings bond is a long time for the economy, and a long time for most people to wait for a return. If you take your money out earlier than the maturity date, the interest penalty will knock down the investment value. If you leave it in during sharp rises in other interest rates, you'll feel you've missed golden opportunities to feather your retirement nest egg.

With the fluctuating-interest method described earlier, CDs allow you to move your money around to take advantage of a rise in interest rates if inflation takes off, or to buy stocks if the market falls and their prices become attractive.

This lack of flexibility is a problem with all long-term investments. You are never sure that the interest rates you're earning are as high as they could become.

So, unless there is a real savings in your effort and a real rate of return that is higher than a more flexible investment, investments in which you must keep your money for a long time aren't the ideal place to park all of your savings.

What would make savings bonds a better deal? If they were tax free. And starting in 1990, they are—but only if the money is to be used for your child's college education. That is a good deal for you and your kids. At current rates,

$1,000 invested in a tax-free savings bond would be worth about $1,450 in five years, $2,050 in 10 years, and $2,900 in 15 years. That compares to a tax-deferred return of $1,300 for five years, $1,750 for 10 years, and $2,400 for 15 years. That's a big difference, and if you have a child going to college five or ten years from now, you should take advantage of the tax-free bonds to pay for their education. But savings bonds shouldn't be the only haven for your retirement savings. They may help retire Uncle Sam's debt, but not you.

CORPORATE AND MUNICIPAL BONDS

You've already been introduced to two kinds of bonds, although you may not have thought of them as such: certificates of deposit and savings bonds. They fall under the classification of debt securities but are just a very small part of it.

This section will deal primarily with two kinds of bonds that are sold by brokerages traded over the counter—corporate bonds and municipal bonds.

As an investor you must learn the difference between a new issue and a bond bought over the counter.

With new issues, the corporation promises to pay you back your principal at the time your bond matures—the par value of the bond, which usually is $1,000. Until maturity, often in 30 years, it pays you interest on a set schedule.

What you buy or sell the bond for between the issue date and the maturity date is up to market forces—other interest rates—and the corporation's or municipality's financial condition. If a business goes bankrupt and is unable to pay off all its debts, then the value of the bond is worth only what the corporation can pay back.

So if you buy a bond at its issue you'll know generally what, when, and how much you'll get back, as long as the company doesn't go bankrupt.

If you buy a bond on the market, meanwhile, you have to do some figuring.

For a bond selling at a market price above its issue price—at a premium— you have to take into account the fact that as the bond's maturity date approaches, its price will go down, even if the bond pays a great interest rate at the premium price. That's because if the bond is to mature soon, its payback will be only for the amount at which it was issued.

What you need to know is the bond yield—the real annual rate of return. You can get that either by obtaining a book that provides the calculations for yields from interest rates and maturity dates or by calling a bond dealer.

A bond selling at a discount will tend to go up in price as it approaches maturity. For example, 30-year bonds with 3 percent and 4 percent interest rates in the early 1960s were selling at about 30 percent of their value a few years ago. Now, as their maturity date approaches, their prices are going up dramatically— reapproaching the $1,000 mark despite low interest. That's because their yields with the promised payment at par are going up. They'll never reach $1,000, but they'll come close.

What that should tell you about bonds with long dates until maturity is this: As interest rates go up, their prices will go down. To match the yields of other securities. Take that into account when buying and selling them.

You also will need to know what extra charge, or premium, a company must pay bond holders to call in its bonds early. This is especially true if you are buying the bond at a premium yourself. Those bonds often carry an initially high interest rate, and that makes it attractive for companies to pay them off early. And if the company premium is less than the premium you paid, such a call could cost you a substantial amount of the money you paid for the bonds—your principal—the worst thing that can happen in planning for retirement.

That makes discounted bonds a safer investment, especially if they are highly rated by rating companies such as Standard & Poor's and Moody's. Bond ratings range from AAA to C and D with the most creditworthy corporations getting AAA ratings.

Low-rated bonds, below Bba, are generally called junk bonds, but they're nothing to turn your nose up at. Junk bond dealer Michael Milken made billions for junk bond investors before being charged with conspiracy by the federal government. The claim against him isn't that investors didn't do well with his advice, but that he tried to do better for himself with inside knowledge.

But *you* can't afford to invest your nest egg in risky deals. If they don't pay off, you can end up busted. Good-quality bonds, though, can be a strong part of your investment mix. They are easily salable, provide a set rate of return, often can be used as collateral for loans, and the principal is usually safer than an investment in stocks.

But the interest on corporate bonds is taxed. And that means you annually lose some of your return, as you do with CDs. Unless, of course, you buy municipal bonds.

Most municipal bonds are tax free. They come in two basic types. General obligation bonds are paid by unspecified tax dollars of the issuing government unit. Revenue bonds are issued to finance specific projects, such as a toll road, bridge, or highway construction. Payment is backed by a particular funding source—gas tax, toll, ticket surcharge (for a municipal stadium), etc.—for the project.

The tax-free nature of such bonds makes them attractive, especially after retirement, but only if the rate is within a range equal to the highest tax rate you pay. If your tax rate is 28 percent, then a tax-free bond at 6.48 percent is about equal to a taxable bond at 9 percent; 6.86 percent tax-free equals 9.5 percent taxable; and 7.2 percent equals 10 percent. But only if the maturity dates and the position—discount or premium—for the different bonds are the same. Compare the yields on these bonds, not merely the rate of return of your investment dollars.

FIXED INCOME INVESTMENTS

These investments provide you regular interest payments by putting their money in long-term debt, such as treasury, municipal and corporate bonds, and mortgage-backed Ginnie Maes.

Sold by brokerage and mutual fund companies, fixed-income investments require a minimum investment that can run from $250 to $10,000, so there's a lot of shopping around for you to do.

Different funds provide different rates of return; and those promising the highest payment often will accomplish this by digging into your principal when interest rates rise and the fund's profits fall. They promise you fixed income, *not* protection of the principal you've invested.

Because of this risk, and because what you're looking for now is an investment that will increase in value until the time you retire, fixed-income investments are better for sustaining your retirement years than building toward them.

TAX-DEFERRED FIXED-RATE ANNUITIES

Tax-deferred fixed-rate annuities suffer from many of the same problems as savings bonds, but not all.

These annuities are contracts with insurance companies. They *aren't* federally insured, but if you choose a good company, the risks are extremely low. Find annuities with companies rated A+ or A by A.M. Best & Co., an insurance-rating service in Oldham, NJ, and you can feel secure your money won't disappear.

Under the annuity contract, between you and the insurance company, the company promises to pay you a set interest rate for a specified period. The rates are adjusted at intervals, some as short as three months and some as long as five years, with market interest rates. That means that you take advantage of the averaging of interest rates over those intervals of adjustments.

You don't need much money to get into them. A $1,000 initial investment is the average, although they range from as little as $500 to as much as $5,000.

Their greatest advantage, as with savings bonds, is that tax on the interest earned in them is deferred; nothing goes to Uncle Sam until the money is withdrawn. And the money can be paid out over time to reduce the tax bite after you retire.

The disadvantage is that you face a 10 percent penalty if you withdraw the money before death, disability, or age 59—in addition to taxes on the interest earned.

The average rate of return over the past five years on these annuities has been about 7.7 percent, which also puts them in a class with savings bonds.

For the lazy or absentminded investor, these annuities are a smart retirement plan. You can habitually put money in them, and the insurance company takes care of the rest: investing, management expertise, rolling the investment over, keeping track of what your savings are doing. You can sit back and relax.

But you won't make as much as you could. And if you have a small retirement savings nest egg to begin with, this kind of annuity won't give you all the money you need when you retire.

You might do better with variable rate annuities.

VARIABLE-RATE ANNUITIES

Unlike the regular annuity with an initial fixed interest rate guaranteed that's then adjusted by the insurance company, a variable-rate annuity provides a menu of mutual funds for you to choose from, including bond and stock and money market funds. After selecting the family of funds you want, then you can switch your money between them to maximize your return. You might split your investment between an income-producing bond fund and a growth-oriented stock fund.

You can do it with a minimum investment of only $1,500 and add as little as $25 at a time.

As with a fixed-rate annuity, you'll be charged a 10 percent penalty and taxed for early withdrawal. On the other hand, you have a tremendous degree of flexibility to take advantage of changes in the economy if you carefully choose the funds you invest in. And you retain the advantage of tax deferral.

What you invest in to build for your retirement isn't the same as what you invest in after you get there. Your pre-retirement concern is financial growth so you'll have an adequate retirement income, not extra income to spend in the present.

And financial growth in our economy means you also must look at mutual funds, stocks, and real estate.

And that's what we'll begin to do in the next few Chapters.

9

Mutual Funds, or The Feeling's Mutual

"This is the Mutual Broadcasting Network." Radio listeners have heard that call filter out of the night sky. Comforting. Warm. Homey. Mutual of Omaha, the insurance company, has the same feel to its name. Friendly and farmbelt.

But when it comes to mutual funds, it can be a wild kingdom out there. It certainly was in the 1960s. Mutuals were "go-go" funds that had investors gah-gah. Pushed by high-pressure salespeople and promoters, they made the junk bond salespeople of today look like choir boys. But when the stock market went bust after elimination of the capital gains tax preference, investors were left gagging on losses, their contributions to their funds gobbled up by sales commissions and management fees that were taken up front. Many were lucky to escape with a dime for every dollar they thought they had invested.

Today's mutuals aren't as wild and wooly as those glorious days of yesteryear. Thank goodness. Regulation helps protect investors much better. There's more reporting required, more explanation before you invest. In fact, with open-ended mutual funds, you must first get a prospectus before you actually buy.

That's good news for you. But it still means you must read and understand the prospectus. (If you buy several funds, you may suffer from prospect-eye, a condition caused by reading too much fine print. But that's better than suffering a bank rupture from loaded funds busting your bank account.)

This Chapter will help give you a *rudimentary* understanding of what mutual funds are and what you can do with them.

Good books such as the *Individual Investor's Guide to No-Load Mutual Funds* by the American Association of Individual Investors and *The Individual Investor's Guide to Closed-End Funds*, both published by International Publishing Corp., 625 N. Michigan, Chicago, IL 60611 can give you loads of information on those kinds of funds, provide annual and five-year performance rankings for the funds, the different funds' portfolios and objectives, and a host of other tips that will make mutual-fund investing easier, safer, and more profitable for you.

Oh, goodie, more reading, you smirk. But think of it this way: At least you won't be aliterate—capable of reading and understanding but not doing so. And you won't be *illiterate* where your money is concerned.

In the interim, while you do that reading and continue to develop your retirement plan, here's some background that will keep you from feeling like a dummy when next you hear at the office, "I just bought an aggressive growth mutual with a no-load through my discount broker, and it promises a 16 percent return on my investment in a year, even after the redemption and after paying the 12b-1."

"Oh, really?" is the normal response to that. All of us like to pretend we know it all. After this, you won't know it *all*, but you *will* know what the guy means. Just don't imitate him.

The first thing to know about mutual funds is why you would ever want to invest in them in the first place.

- **Instant diversification.** To invest *individually* in the stocks or bonds of most mutual funds and achieve equal diversification would cost $50,000. That's a lot of cash just to take advantage of averaging slices of those markets, or whole markets themselves. Averaging means you don't gain the total rewards if you choose one particular high-powered stock, but it also means you don't risk the total loss of your nest egg if that one stock goes bust. Because mutual funds, which essentially are investment syndicates, buy shares across a spectrum of stocks, and you buy a share that includes the spectrum they invest in, you are diversified, and that can help you find your retirement pot of gold.

- **Cheap management expertise.** Mutual fund managers are experts in the investing they do. Thus, when you buy a share, you are buying that expertise. The only cost can often be management fees paid through the profits of the fund. Those tend to be small fractions of the total, so you are getting cheap advice. And if you choose a mutual fund wisely, the advice you get won't leave you feeling you have to be a cheapskate in retirement.

- **Quick change.** You can often shift your investments from one kind to another within a particular fund group at no cost or low cost. That makes managing your portfolio easier and potentially more profitable. If economic conditions change, you can change with them—without the fees and commissions you must pay if you owned separate, individual investments that you would have to buy and sell singly.

- **Easy reinvestment.** Most funds let you take all your dividend or capital gain distributions and use them to buy extra shares of the fund, including fractional shares, which you can then sell as needed. For income funds, this can be useful if you put your shares in a tax-exempt IRA or a 401(K) plan. You can shift your investments in those plans between different funds and maximize (or, in English, make the most of) your investment in those plans.

- **Easy recordkeeping.** Compared to most other kinds of investments, the records you'll need to keep for tax purposes with mutual funds are a snap. You don't even have to hold stock certificates as you do with stocks you buy—the fund will do that for you. The one thing you'll need to do is keep track of the blocks of funds you buy and sell. We'll get into that in our discussion of investment recordkeeping in Chapter 13.

- **Simple dollar-cost averaging.** As with stocks, you can buy a set dollar amount in a mutual fund each month and thus take advantage of dollar-cost averaging—buying the most shares when prices are down and the least when prices for the fund are high.

With all those advantages, there has got to be a downside to mutual funds. Otherwise, why would anyone *not* invest in one?

Well, for the super-involved investor, mutual funds allow manipulation, but they don't allow you to play the hunches you might like in the market. They are not set up for big killings but for making your money work to keep you ahead of inflation.

Another problem is that some of the charges for mutual funds can be confusing. With a broker, you know you're paying for his services with each transaction, but mutual funds seem to involve a series of charges throughout their lifetime. They're needed to pay the managers of the funds—without whom a fund would not exist—but the way they are paid coupled with how distributions are set for the fund's proceeds to investors make mutual funds more confusing to many investors than stocks or bonds.

Finally, if you invest in the wrong mutual fund at the wrong time, you can lose a lot of money.

That, though, is true for any kind of investment. And unless you plan to be super-involved in managing your investment portfolio, the only real inhibition about mutual funds is the confusion you might feel about what they do and how they operate. Here's some information to dispel that cloud.

HOW MUTUAL FUNDS OPERATE

Mutual funds are of two main types both of which can be subdivided into eight subgroups.

The two types are closed-end funds and open-end funds.

A *closed-end fund* has a set number of shares that does not change. Once shares are sold, the fund manager then invests the proceeds. Profits from those investments are then divided up among the fund's shareholders, less the manager's fee. The fund's underlying value is the asset value of the investments. But market demand determines the value of those shares, too. If the return on those assets isn't as much as can be made from investments in other assets, the price of the share in the fund will drop until investors find the return attractive enough for them to invest. If the return on those assets is higher, the price of a share will rise until the return to the last new shareholders to buy equals what they could get elsewhere.

The only way to buy shares of closed-ended funds is to get them from a shareholder, and the proceeds from these exchanges do nothing to increase the value of the fund. They flow strictly between the buyer and the seller of the shares. These funds are, in that respect, much like stocks or bonds sold on the market.

An *open-end fund*, on the other hand, is authorized to sell a certain number of shares, but they exceed the number of outstanding shares. Thus the fund continues to sell new shares which then go to buy new assets. A shareholder in the fund doesn't sell his shares on the open market but sells them back to the fund for their net asset value, less any management fee that is applied. That fee must be spelled out when you buy into the fund. As such, the asset pool for an open-end fund increases when new shares are issued and decreases when shares are sold back to the fund. The value of a share of an open-end fund is strictly tied to the value and profitability of its assets, not to the supply and demand for shares.

Closed-end funds have the advantage of being sold easily through the stock market. And the investment cost to you is the same as for stocks—a broker's fee when you buy it and when it is sold.

Open-ended funds may be bought through brokerage houses and sold there. They may be bought and sold directly by the fund. The fee structure, though, for an open-end fund is different from that of a closed-end fund.

You want to buy $1,000 of Hazardous Mutual Super Growth that has a 16 percent growth rate. You go to your broker and he tells you sure, great buy. You plunk down $1,000.

Have you just invested $1,000? Not if it is a front-end load fund. The load—a sale's commission—goes to the broker. It could be anywhere from 4 percent to the more traditional 8.5 percent. And it comes out up front. With an 8.5 percent front-end load, what you get is not a $1,000 investment but a $915 investment. That's what your investment will grow from at 16 percent.

The *real* charge amounts to $85 over that $915 ($85 divided by $915), or 9.3 percent, not 8.5 percent. And it will take that fund 11 years to beat an investment earning a full percentage point less—which also is probably less risky for you—that doesn't have that load. The $915 at 16 percent will be worth $4,682 then, versus $4,652 for the no-load fund at 15 percent. And that's only if that fund can hold its advantage through the whole 11 years, which is unlikely. You take your money out any earlier, though, and you'd be sure to make less.

The front-end load, though, isn't the only kind of fee.

Some funds have redemptions or back-end loads they charge you on the way out. And other funds charge you through the course of your investment, assessed annually, with what are called 12b-1 plan charges. Those charges are legitimate if they pay for distribution, printing, and mailing prospectus and other actual costs for operating the fund. But they can be loaded up to provide sales commissions for brokers.

A 0.1 percent 12b-1 charge is no big deal—it would amount to only a 1 percent front-end load after 10 years. But a full 1 percent 12b-1 charge is a big deal. It would be more than the traditional 8.5 percent front-end load after 10 years. In fact, it would be equal to a 10 percent front-end load then, rising to 20 percent at 20 years.

Those are the fees you have to look out for when you invest in a mutual fund. That doesn't mean you shouldn't invest, if the manager of the fund is really outstanding and the fund historically keeps beating other funds by enough percentage points to cover the fees. But that usually isn't the case. So be careful out there. Especially, since with a little investigation, you usually can find a fund with *no-load* and low fees that is equal to the fund with the fees and the loads.

Good funds should sell themselves; they shouldn't need high sales commissions to get others to push them.

As important as finding a fund with low fees is finding the right kind of fund for your temperament and your investment objectives. What you need is what you should invest in.

CATEGORIES OF MUTUAL FUNDS

They have all kinds of names, but they fit generally into eight categories:

- **Aggressive Growth Funds.** These funds invest aggressively in common stocks, often in emerging companies or companies deemed undervalued but ready to grow with a shift in the economy's needs. The managers of these funds will borrow money, trade stock options, and buy and sell stock index futures to achieve aggressive growth. They aren't into income production at all—not from interest or dividends. They want to build up unrealized—and untaxed until realized—capital gains. During bull markets, they shine. But in bear markets, you'll lose your stomach on this roller coaster. The key is to hang on through the full economic and market cycle. If you're willing to sit through the ride over 10 to 15 years, you can have spectacular results—much better than with most other kinds of investments.

- **Growth Funds.** They have the same aim as aggressive growth funds, only without as many hair-raising shenanigans. They invest in more established growth companies—Apple Computer at 10 to 15 years of age, not at two or three. They'll build up cash during uncertain times to tide them over downward swings. They'll still follow the market, but not as steeply—more like swinging from the Blue Ridge Mountains to the Shenandoah Valley than aggressive-growth leaps from Pike's Peak to Death Valley in a bear market. Some of them even can run counter to market trends. Picking up some of them along with an aggressive growth fund can diversify you through the whole range of growth stocks.

- **Growth and Income Funds.** They are going for what amounts to a mix of capital gains and dividend income. They primarily invest in stocks that pay good dividends and may even invest in some preferred stocks and in bonds. Public utility common stocks, which tend to increase their returns with inflation, are usually part of these funds' portfolios. Overall, these funds do better in a declining market, but investors should try to shelter the distributions from these funds as they are frequent and fully taxable. This is a fund for your individual retirement account or 401(K) plan, if you have one.

- **Balanced Funds.** The line between these and growth and income funds is becoming blurred. It used to be that balanced funds allocated a fixed proportion of their assets to stocks and bonds. They will now state the proportion intended in their prospectus. But, nowadays it often is variable, with the promise by the managers that the fund is seeking the maximum "total return" on assets. That makes them not much different than growth and income funds. And like growth and income funds, their high-dividend yields mean they should be sheltered in tax-exempt accounts where possible. There, the dividends can be reinvested to build up your retirement account.

- **Bond Funds.** As the name says, these funds invest in bonds, rather than stocks. That doesn't mean they should automatically be salted away in an IRA or 401(K) plan. Different funds specialize in different kinds of bonds. Some funds specialize in municipal bonds, sometimes geared to different states. Those bond funds don't need a tax-sheltered account as they are tax free at the federal level and may be tax free at the state and local level where you live if they are targeted to your state. Other bonds, such as funds that invest in low-rated, corporate bonds—junk bonds—are risky. You might take a loss on them. And if you do, you'll want to deduct that from your income tax, something you can't do with a bond salted away in an IRA or 401(K) plan. Realizing that you may have losses to go along with gains in investing in junk bonds, you might be better advised to pay tax on their high yields and put safer, steadier investments into your sheltered accounts. One thing you'll want to check in buying a bond fund is the maturity date. Many are short-term, which means the bonds in the portfolio have an average maturity of three years. Others are long-term, which means over ten years. The longer the term, the greater the risk and the greater should be the return. But remember—a long-term bond paying 4 percent in the 1960s was a great return then. It is piddling today, and it was piddling in the 1970s. Just make sure you don't lock all your money—and all your tax shelter—into long-term bonds. They may lose value if rates go higher, and selling them at a loss at retirement doesn't do you a lot of good. Overall, though, bond funds are less risky than stock-based funds. They are worse at providing growth but better at providing income. They are what you may want to move into as you move closer to retirement or into retirement, when your tolerance for risk goes down and your need for income rises.

- **Precious Metal Funds.** These funds allow you to invest in gold and other precious metals such as platinum and silver without the joy of getting the actual metal and caressing it. Such funds are inflation hedges, just as the metals are. They fluctuate with the worries and fears of people about inflation. Buy them if you want, but don't bet on them providing for your retirement.

- **International Funds.** These give you a chance to invest in foreign countries. The problem: Not only do these fluctuate with economic conditions in those countries, their rate of return depends on the currency exchange rate between it and the United States. If you buy when the dollar is strong and sell when it is weak, you're golden. Do it the other way around, and you're dirt. Imagine investing in Japanese investments when the dollar sold for 220 yen and then selling when the dollar sold for 125 yen two years later. What a return! But if you bought at 125 yen and sold at 145 yen, what a disaster.

- **Cash Reserve Funds.** I talked about these earlier. They are money market funds. They are best as a quick place to put your money not as your retirement nest egg. Many provide check-writing privileges if you keep a minimum in the account. They aren't federally insured, like CDs and a bank account, but they are pretty safe and very liquid so you can make other investments from them with ease.

So what kind of mutual fund should you get? A variety.

How you weight your investments will depend on how much time you have left until retirement, how much you'll need when you get there, what tolerance you have for risk, and what market and economic conditions are when you make your investment.

Mutual funds can help diversify you to reduce risk, but they don't eliminate it. They react to economic conditions as do other investments. Some in different ways. I told you about some of the risks when I described each kind of mutual fund category.

But different funds within the groups have different characteristics, too. To find out how they react to changing conditions, get their prospectus and get some books that provide track records of other funds. Don't look at just one.

Before you invest, read through the Condensed Financial Information Statement of the prospectus. Investment income gives you the dividends and interest earned by the fund in a given year. Expenses reflect the management costs of the fund. Net investment income equals investment income minus expenses—that will tell you how stable the fund is over time. Net realized and unrealized capital gains and losses tell you how the value of the fund's investments that have been bought or sold have changed. If you're interested in growth, their track record is vitally important to you. Net asset value changes can have many causes—increased distributions to shareholders being one. A decline doesn't necessarily mean poor performance. The expense ratio is important. A fund spending more than 2 percent of its net asset value on expenses is expensive. The average is 1.25 percent. The ratio of net investment income to net assets should be close to 0 percent for aggressive growth funds, close to 3 percent for growth and income funds. Finally, the portfolio turnover rate will give you a clue how foresighted your manager is in picking good investments. The average turnover rate is between 80 percent and 100 percent. A high rate suggests sensitivity to changing conditions. That's the norm for aggressive growth funds and some bond funds. A low rate indicates a more stable income fund—more blue chip companies. Who's going to sell IBM?

The prospectus of a fund also will tell you what fees are charged, how you can buy, and how you can redeem your shares.

So, get prospect-eye, get some guides to make comparisons, and then choose some mutual funds in which to invest. And then set up a schedule to make those investments—not all at once in one fund, but gradually into several.

And while you're doing that, you also can decide whether you'd like to jump into stocks—the subject of the next Chapter.

10

Stock Investing, or Have You Seen a Cute Equity Lately?

There's no use kidding yourself. If you want to make money for your retirement, at some point you'll have to invest in the stock market.

To many people, that's a scary proposition. Stocks, after all, are associated with Black Monday and Black Friday. They feature creatures called Bulls and others called Bears. They go boom or they go crash. And they are filled with jargon, such as puts and calls and options and selling short and selling long and, that most fearful of all, a margin call.

You've got to be nuts to invest in the stock market. But then, America's a crazy place. It's filled with jittery investors. And you should be one of them.

First, though, let's get rid of some of the mystery about stocks. They aren't exactly like a crap shoot in Vegas or roulette in Atlantic City. They aren't all a gamble or a big stakes game. They are an investment. And what you are investing in is business. If you think business is going to go bad, don't invest. If you think business will go on, do.

A share of stock is a certificate of ownership in a business. It is a share that at some time the company issued at a certain value, its par value, and now is traded among the public.

In a total sale of the company's assets, it guarantees you a piece of what's left after the bank, bondholders, preferred shareholders, and a couple others get their pieces. But since the assets of most companies are worth more than their accumulated debts and almost double the value of their outstanding stock in most cases, you've got a piece of paper that's worth more than the ink it's printed on. Which is more than can be said for the faith and credit backing Uncle Sam's notes.

Still, you don't buy stock anticipating a fire sale. A takeover, maybe, or a big merger, but not a bargain basement fire sale. You buy a stock because you think a company will grow, increase its dividends, increase its assets, improve its stock price, and make you money.

And that happens an awful lot.

Sure, you can read about the USA having 600,000 bankruptcies each year. But how many of those are in publicly traded companies? Most companies make profits. Most companies pay dividends. Most companies reinvest and buy new assets. They grow not merely with the U.S. economy but with the world economy. And there's one fact about that economy—it hasn't stopped growing since the start of the dark ages.

Even during the 1970s in this country—with gas lines, inflation, unemployment—the economy grew. We had recessions when we stopped for a little while. But then we grew again.

LOOK LONG TERM

The key in looking at stocks and the economy is to think not short term, but long term.

You have to. Most stocks, except certain blue chip varieties, don't pay dividends equal to what you can get in interest from CDs, or money market funds, or Savings Bonds. What you are looking for is their potential to grow.

Unlike bonds and most other investments, stocks increase in value as the assets underlying them grow in worth. And as a company grows, its dividends should increase.

Thus, if you buy a company's stock at $25 a share and it gives a dividend of $1.25 a share, your initial return is only 5 percent, which is not uncommon.

But if the company grows 10 percent a year—also not uncommon—its next dividend increases to $1.37 a share, a 5.5 percent return. And it grows another 10 percent, and the dividend increases to $1.51 a share, then to $1.66, then to $1.83, then to $2.01, then to $2.21. And during that same period, the value of the company's stock rises—to $27.50, to $30.25, to $33.28, to $36.61, to $40.27, to $44.30.

In looking at stocks, you have to combine that dividend payout and the increase in the stock's price to determine its value. And then determine the after-tax return.

The dividend part of its value is taxable, like most interest. The growth in the price of the stock is like the tax-deferred interest of a U.S. Savings Bond or an annuity, or money earned in an Individual Retirement Account. You only pay taxes on it at the time you sell the stock.

That's why if you invest in stocks to create a retirement nest egg, rather than income right now, you're interested more in those that pay lower dividends but grow in value at above average rates than in those that give you a high dividend. You want them to increase the value of your investment, tax deferred, so you will have more when you retire.

The one troubling thing about stocks is that they don't always increase in a straight line. You stand the chance of losing your money. That's why stock investors are jittery. There's always the possibility of recession for the economy or bankruptcy for a company. There's always the chance that you bought a stock at its world high and will never see it reach that peak again.

But the rewards of stock investments for long-term investors on average beat other kinds of investments. The most basic thing you should think about if you invest in a particular stock is that you are, in effect, buying a business.

What would you look for in a business you'd like to buy? Here's a list:

- The demand or need for products it sells.

- The quality of its management.

- Its reputation.

- Its present profits.

- Its prospects for future growth.

- Its products or activities interest you.

The first five points are pretty plain. The last deserves some explanation.

Think for a minute: If you were to involve yourself in a business that bores you, you probably wouldn't do very well in it. So, why buy stock in companies that don't interest you?

Your edge in investing is your interest. And money interest alone won't give you that edge. After all, if you aren't interested in either the personalities running a business or its product lines, are you going to want to read about it?

And that's what you'll have to do if you invest in individual stocks. You'll have to read about the company, its financial situation, how its products are doing. If you find it interesting, that's a lot easier to do.

But how do you *know* you'll be interested in a company? Well, what interests *you*? If you're interested in computers, it's likely you'll have some interest in the companies that make or supply them. If you have an interest in fishing, the facts about the company that makes rods and reels could fascinate you. If you're concerned about energy conservation, businesses that are involved in recycling or the development of new energy-efficient materials might hold your attention.

The United States has hundreds of industries to choose from—entertainment, publishing, communications, automobiles, steel and paper products, drugs, chemicals, energy, resorts, fast food.

If you have just a little curiosity about any of these industries, choose a couple and investigate the companies that are doing things in them. That's one good way to start investing in stocks. From your own personal interest, for your own personal interest.

What do you look for? Well, find out about the products or services in the industry—do they sell well all the time, do better in a boom economy and go bust in a bad one or vice versa (some food companies and utilities do best in bad times)? The business cycle and the cyclical nature of some businesses tell you whether now is a good time to invest in them.

Is the industry fresh, with a lot of competitors, or mature, with just a few? Picking a good company in an industry that is just starting to grow can get you higher rates of growth in deferred-tax stock value as opposed to taxable dividends. New technology or new kinds of services provide the greatest possibility for growth.

CHOOSING YOUR INVESTMENT COMPANY

Once you've decided what kind of industry you're investing in, then you can start looking at companies within them.

In addition to picking companies whose products or services you like, you'll want to look at the fundamentals of how various companies in that industry operate. That means looking at their financial data.

You can find much of that out at the library—going through issues of *Barron's*, *Business Week*, *Financial World*, *The Wall Street Journal*, and a number of other sources.

Or you can write the companies for their most recent annual report and the Form 10K it must file as a publicly traded company.

The first thing you look at is a company's balance sheet. Just like your balance sheet, a corporate balance sheet is divided between assets, current and long term, and liabilities. The company's assets will equal its liabilities plus its stockholders' equity. And the sheet will divide that equity by the number of shares outstanding to provide the book value for the firm.

Book value is important, because it tells you whether the value underlying the stock reflects the price you're being asked to pay for it on the market. That's because stockholders' equity is equal to original stockholder investment in the company plus the earnings the company retains after paying dividends to stockholders.

The balance sheet also will tell you indirectly whether the company is strapped for cash or fairly liquid. If its cash and other current assets aren't double its current liabilities, then it could face some cash problems in the near future that will force it to borrow money and limit future dividends or growth.

After the balance sheet, you look at the income statement. It will give you the company's net profit figure. Divide that by the number of shares outstanding and you get the company's earnings per share. And from the earnings per share, you can find out its price-earnings (P/E) ratio by dividing the earnings per share by the current stock price in the newspaper. The higher the number, the lower the earnings per share—and the lower the return on investment.

A high P/E stock, though, may not be a bad investment. If a company has taken on debt to build a new plant or decided to forego profit to wipe out an old debt, the company's P/E might drop dramatically in the next year as its profits increase. That's where your interest in the industry and the businesses within it will make a difference, because you'll read about those things while many other investors will only look at numbers.

After checking these items, though, you'll want to check the companies you're investigating against each other. And you'll want to find out some history on how their stocks have been trading. Is one company selling at an historic high while another is selling at a low? Has any one company's sales been increasing faster than others over the past few quarters?

Keeping abreast of these things is why you had better be interested in the industry you're investing in. You can make good money doing it. You, in fact, can reap much larger rewards than other investors. But any flagging of your interest could lead to losing a lot of money as well.

HOW TO HEDGE YOUR BETS

There's a way to hedge your bets, so to speak. You can write options. This is a conservative investment strategy.

What you do is simply inform your broker that you want to write an option on the stock you hold. A buyer for the option will be found who will offer to buy the stock for a certain price, paying a premium for that option. If the price of the stock goes above that price, then you have to sell the option buyer the stock for the agreed-upon price. You get the premium and the selling price, minus a seller's commission. The buyer gets a quick profit on the stock, minus the premium and buyer's commission. If the stock doesn't rise, you get the premium and the buyer gets nothing. This kind of option is a call.

The process works in reverse if you think the stock will fall below a certain level. Then you buy an option and pay a premium to somebody who agrees to buy the stock for that price in a certain time frame. If the stock falls, the person you've paid the premium to must buy the stock at the agreed-upon price. If the stock doesn't fall, you're out the premium, but at least your stock hasn't lost value. This kind of option is called a put.

There are numerous other methods of hedging in this area. They are basically for people who really want to be active in the market and like the action, not for people seeking to establish a portfolio of investments for their retirement. They are short-term strategies for making money in the market.

Long-term strategies for retirement mean you must overlook the short-term fluctuations of price. You must investigate the company and industry you're investing in and plan on holding stocks through market swings. You must avoid thinking about hot buys and think about the underlying value of a stock.

Once you've done that, then you can plant certain hedges in your stock portfolio.

How? Take advantage of dollar-cost averaging. This basically amounts to putting specified amounts of money each month or each quarter in stocks on your list. It amounts to doing with stocks what you did with CDs—averaging out the price and return by spreading your purchases over time.

Dollar-cost averaging buys fewer shares when the market is high and more when the market is low. It takes advantage of the overall trend in the economy, which is toward continued growth, and within an industry that is high growth.

This spread also works to your advantage should you choose to sell some stocks if you need cash. You can sell those you bought at the higher prices and not pay as much tax. Or if you sell them at a loss, you can take a capital loss of up to $3,000 a year on your income tax, reducing your tax bite. At the same time, the stocks you bought low will continue to retain value and grow to provide for your retirement.

The other reasons you might choose to sell would be that you consider your stock and the whole market tremendously overpriced, as occurred before the stock market crash of October 1987. Or you don't like the direction a company you've invested in is taking—it's started to go bad. Again, your interest in an industry and company will give you an edge in getting out before other investors who only look at numbers.

The biggest hedge, though, is to spread your money around. Don't invest in just one company, or one industry. Choose several.

If you can, split up your investments between cyclical and counter-cyclical businesses and between growth and income companies. Combine that strategy with dollar-cost averaging your investments in them and you will reduce your risk even more. For in-depth information on market watching and stock analysis, consult *Do-It-Yourself Investment Analysis: A Practical Guide to Life Cycle, Fundamental and Technical Analysis* by James Burgauer (IPC, 625 N. Michigan, Chicago, IL 60611).

To sum up a stock market investment strategy:

1. Select industries that interest you to put your savings in.

2. Pick companies within those industries based upon your reading about their management, products, and operations.

3. Compare their book value to stock price, their ratio of current assets to current liabilities, and their ratio of stock price to the net income per share (the price to earnings ratio).

4. Check each company's history of dividend payments and stock price.

5. Invest for the long-term, using dollar-cost averaging to take advantage of market swings so your investment will grow with the trend in the industry.

6. Diversify your stock holdings among different companies and different industries.

7. Keep up-to-date on the companies and industries you invest in. That way you will know when to get out.

If all this sounds like too much for you, don't forget that there's still a way to invest in the stock market and make money for your retirement. It doesn't bring you the potential of as large returns as this plan would. But you won't have to put quite as much effort into it. That investment strategy is mutual funds, the area explored in the previous Chapter.

11

Real Estate, or the Land of False Retirement Hopes

"Land. It's the only thing you can count on." Or so said Papa O'Hara to young Scarlett.

But if you watched *Gone With The Wind* closely, you noticed that to keep her beloved Tara, Scarlett had to scheme, to lie, to cheat. She had to bring money in from outside sources. She had to work like the devil to keep Tara alive.

And what did Tara do? Well, the minute it was neglected, it didn't do a dang thing. It deteriorated, became weed covered, developed leaks in the roof.

The good earth of Tara had problems with location, too. It was in the South at the wrong time.

Papa O'Hara should have added, "You can count on it to be a big headache." But, no, he was a bit more dramatic: "It's the only thing that's worth fightin' and dyin' for."

Maybe it comes from our agricultural roots, our desire to own a piece of property. And the only real property is land and buildings. None of that fake stuff, like a stock certificate or a bond paper. Whatever the reason, though, people have been fightin' and dyin' with real estate for centuries.

There is the belief that real estate is the way to get rich. There is a false notion among many, though, that if you own a lot of land and property, you are rich.

Well, that isn't necessarily so. Many farmers found that out in the early 1980s. Speculation in land was high in the 1970s because of inflation, so farmers borrowed a lot of money on inflated land values for new equipment and to expand their farms. But when inflation ebbed, they were caught in a squeeze. The extra land many of them bought couldn't produce enough income from crops to sustain the costs they incurred to buy it and the extra equipment to work it. So, many of these land-rich farmers ended up dirt poor.

Real estate values depend on what can be gotten out of them—their rental or income value. That's true not only for farmland but for apartment buildings, single-family housing, office complexes, factories, shopping centers.

A booming economy tends to push up real estate prices because it increases incomes and the ability of people or businesses to pay higher rents. The boom doesn't have to be national. It can be local. That's what happened in Texas. Spurred by the oil industry, real estate prices rose fast, encouraging more and more investment in real estate projects. Savings and loan managers got caught in the fever. But when the oil economy went bad, people started defaulting on real estate loans. Their incomes couldn't support the rental values.

That's why looking at real estate as a one-way ticket to wealth is foolish. There are limits to what people can afford. And if what people can afford goes down, real estate prices must go down, too.

YOUR HOME AS A RETIREMENT NEST EGG

One reason you should not look upon your home as your retirement nest egg is because of this uncertainty about real estate values in any given place at any given time.

Imagine the plight of Houston retirees when prices for their homes went down in their city—they had planned to use their homes as a fund for their retirement in 1988. Or of home owners in some of the towns where military bases are expected to close. Or in neighborhoods that have become blighted. Or even in some booming areas, if their home wasn't the right type for the people moving into the area.

And what happens to your retirement nest egg if you decide to stay put? The only way it can generate income then is if you take a loan against the equity you own in it—in essence selling it back to the bank.

Your home should not be counted on as the major source of your savings. And you shouldn't count it as a real estate investment for retirement purposes. Instead, you should count retirement investments only those real estate ventures you buy to produce income through rents, dividends, or capital gains.

To make money through direct investment and personal ownership of real estate, you need to buy property that is in the right place, at the right time, at the right price. And that isn't an easy thing to do.

Not that real estate investments are bad. There are advantages. You usually can leverage a lot of money with small down payments, often only 20 percent of the value of the property you're buying. You can depreciate buildings and equipment on your property for tax purposes, usually at a faster rate than they actually deteriorate. You can deduct interest and other expenses. You can hold on to the real estate for a long time without it costing you a thing if you can find a good rental use for it—grazing or camping on undeveloped land, office or housing rents on developed pieces. And if you buy a good piece of property and develop it properly, you can make a lot of money.

But it won't come easy. It will take a lot of hard work. And it can strap you for cash that might go into other kinds of investments. Real estate isn't quickly or easily turned into cash like a stock or a bond. It can take months and sometimes even years to sell. And while down payments may be small percentagewise, they are big in dollar terms. A minimum of $7,500 for a place selling for $37,500. More than $18,000 for a median-priced home.

BASIC CONSIDERATIONS

But if you're still interested, here are some basic considerations in buying property:

- **Location.** Is the property in an area that is increasing in value or declining after inflation is taken into account? If going up after inflation, has it been on an upward trend for a long time or just started recently? You don't want to buy property where values are going down or might go down in the future. You are looking for an upswing, so recent trends are more important. Look for a property in an area where prices are starting to draw even with inflation. That can signal greater appreciation in the future.

- **Transformation.** Can the property be improved or its use changed? The key to making money in real estate is to turn a piece of property to its highest income-producing use at its location. You gain most if you take a piece of property and buy it for a price with a lower income-producing use and transform it in to a higher use. For example, if you can buy a house used as a single-family residence and can transform it to a duplex without harming the character of the neighborhood, you can increase its income production and make the property worth more. Whether you can do so will depend upon local zoning ordinances, opposition by neighbors to exceptions in zoning, and the cost of conversion. Remember: Most developers make their wealth not from buying and holding a piece of property, but by improving it—putting it to a higher income-producing use.

- **Competition.** How many other people are converting their properties to uses similar to the one you want? If many are, the market may become glutted and your rents will go down. You might then think of a compatible use for your property that will take advantage of their competition—a small group of stores next to an area glutted by apartments, an interior decorator shop, or a doctor's office.

- **Price.** How does a property's price compare with others in the area and with prices of similar places in other areas? You pay too much, you'll get back too little.

- **Costs.** What will be your cost of maintaining and improving the property? A cheap piece of real estate that you'll have to sink your life's savings into improvements or conversion often won't pay off.

- **Income.** What will you make on this property and how does the return compare with other kinds of investments? To answer these questions, you will need to:

  1. estimate current and future rental income;

  2. estimate current and future expenses, including the interest cost of borrowing the money to buy the property;

  3. determine how long you plan to own the property;

  4. forecast a sales price (using past price increases of similar properties in adjoining areas).

To find all this out, you'll have to gather sales records, work with contractors, and hire an accountant and a lawyer. It won't be, as one contractor told me when he went to fix my plumbing and then swore a blue streak through the leaks, "a piece of cake." That's why I wouldn't recommend it to everyone.

Especially since you don't have to do that to invest in real estate. There are other ways.

REAL ESTATE INVESTMENT TRUSTS

REITs are primarily real estate mutual funds. What a REIT does is buy and manage real estate, with 90 percent of its income going back to investors in the form of dividends. REITs tend to outperform the housing market—housing prices in the last five years of the 1980s went up about 25 percent while REITs increased in value by more than 60 percent on average. They underperformed the stock market in that period, as it nearly doubled, but they are less volatile than stocks.

REITs don't have the tax advantages associated with the actual buying and selling of real estate. But they don't have the headaches either. You don't have to be on call for renters' complaints, go out on a limb to meet an extra mortgage, or raise $10,000, $20,000, $30,000, or more for a down payment.

You also don't have to hire professionals to help run your properties. As with mutual funds, you get built-in expertise when you buy into a REIT.

As with a closed-end mutual fund, you can buy and sell REITs on the stock exchange or in the over-the-counter market. As with all investments except tax-exempt mutual funds, you pay taxes on your dividends while the REIT itself pays no corporate taxes. And as with mutual funds, you can choose different REITs with different objectives and portfolios and purchase shares with as little as $500.

Some REITs seek high appreciation in real estate values. Others emphasize income over appreciation. Some invest in certain kinds of real estate—shopping centers, office buildings, apartment complexes, hotels, or other income-producing property. Others invest in a range of real estate investments. Some invest nationally, others in specific regions.

Before buying a REIT, you have to decide how much risk you're willing to take. REITs that invest in specific sectors or regions provide the greatest potential for big gains but they also offer the most risk because the economy in that sector or region might turn sour. Those that invest nationally will have lower gains, but less risk because they are more diversified.

As with a mutual fund, one key you can look at is management. Good management seeks to:

- **get consistent returns.** If returns are up and down, that may indicate a management is just along to ride on your money and the economy rather than making money work through strategic investments.

- **sell property at a profit.** A good consistent record of profitable sales even during bad times shows a management that is aware of market conditions and investor's needs.

- **limit its debt.** If a REIT's debts are higher than 50 percent of it assets, your investment can go sour quickly in a recession—especially if the REIT is heavily invested in a particular industry or region.

Things to look for in a REITs performance are its earnings per share. A good REIT will have earnings per share that beat inflation 1½ times the rate—double the inflation rate is even better. And it should have been able to beat inflation consistently over the past five years. If you find one that does, and the price of a share when divided by its earnings is less than the price-earnings ratio for the Standard & Poor's 500 ratio, investing in that REIT will be better than investing in a broadly invested growth mutual fund.

And if times are inflationary—with the Consumer Price Index rising more than 5 percent a year—equity REITs can provide some protection as management can raise rents and pass them on to investors as higher dividends even as the properties themselves appreciate in value.

Watch out, though, in inflationary times. Mortgage REITs' prices will fall along with interest rates just as bond prices do because they are a fixed-income security. Mortgage REITs do best when prices rise less than 5 percent. Still, like O'Hara's land, a REIT may be something you can count on.

LIMITED PARTNERSHIPS

This form of passive investment in real estate used to be popular because of the tax write-offs it provided.

Primarily, what limited partnerships do is pool money to buy properties. A sponsor organizes them—sometimes a big investment group such as E.F. Hutton—and acts as the general partner that manages the investment. Those who invest in the "units" owned by the partnership are called limited partners.

The general partner handles the buying, managing, and selling of properties, usually investing the money into a particular kind of venture. For example, the GP may buy apartment buildings, office complexes, shopping malls, or industrial properties, choosing some in several locations to defray risk.

Money from rents plus tax deductions for expenses are passed on to the investors. Before tax reform those deductions used to be the key to limited partnerships. They could be used to offset an individual's salary income. Now, they can be used only to offset the income from passive investments, so the key now for partnerships is income production.

In addition to income, partners also get the proceeds from the sale of assets at the end of the partnership, which is usually after seven to 12 years.

It is that long period of ownership that makes limited partnerships a risky deal. Many people can't afford to have their money tied up for that long. And most units sell for $5,000—although a unit that will go into an individual retirement account may be bought for $1,000. The general partner has no obligation to buy back a unit, as is the case with a mutual fund. So, you may have to sell the unit at a discount if you need the cash.

Often LPs have high fees—up to 20 percent up front. And if they don't take it up front, they may charge large management and commission fees at the time of sale.

If you decide to invest, what you'll need to do is make sure the limited partnership you hook in with has a long track record of successful deals. And the best way to do that is through a broker who keeps track of them.

Ask the broker, though, to check the Stanger Offering Terms Ranking. Robert A. Stanger & Co. of Shrewsbury, NJ (201-389-3600), tracks most public partnerships and rates them in terms of quality with a AAA+ going to the ones that put more of your dollars into the investment rather than into fees.

You need to be leery of partnerships that promise overly high yields; they may be returning some of your investment capital to you.

That's especially true of equipment-leasing limited partnerships. Unlike real estate limited partnerships, the assets of equipment-leasing limited partnerships depreciate in value over the time of the investment. If you invest $10,000 at the beginning and get 20 percent yield—$2,000 a year—you'll have earned $14,000 over seven years. But because the equipment depreciated over that time and was sold for only $2,000, you'll get back only $2,000 of your initial investment. That's $16,000, or only a 7 percent real return over the entire term.

Limited partnerships aren't limited to real estate and equipment. If you're interested in becoming a movie producer, invest in a movie production partnership, although most of those don't provide much return. Even those with some blockbuster hits. Other LPs are involved in oil and gas, cable TV, research and development or in commodities.

This latter group—commodities limited partnerships—are actually the commodities market's equivalent of mutual funds. Like the commodities market, though, it is a roller coaster ride if you buy one. Commodity funds jumped 41 percent in 1987, but they had negative growth in 1988.

The minimum purchase, as with an LP, is $5,000. They have high fees, up to 25 percent of your investment. They can be tracked only by calling your broker or buying the *Managed Account Report* newsletter at 5513 Twin Knolls Road, Suite 213, Columbia, MD, 21045 for $225 a year.

To get in, you have to buy a new issue—which you can find through your broker or the newsletter. Once in, you have to give written notice before leaving and can do so only quarterly or monthly, depending on the fund.

If you get in, though, the best advice is to stay in through the wild ride. Most of these funds are designed to dissolve if losses reach 50 percent. Although some dissolve at 30 percent. If you're losing already and have to wait to sell anyway, you probably can't lose much more, and the fund might just suddenly zoom up.

With all limited partnerships, you have to be prepared to see them through. That's why if you don't have a lot saved, investing in them might be better left until you do. And then when you do, don't put anymore than 10 percent of any of your savings into a particular limited partnership.

After all, these real estate investments aren't worth fightin' and dyin' for.

But being prepared for the fightin' and the dyin', well that's something you should plan for, and it's part of the next Chapter.

12

Building and Protecting Your Portfolio

Kenny Rogers had it right: You've got to know when to hold 'em, know when to fold 'em. Know when to walk away, know when to run.

Professional gamblers know those rules. They know they have to play the odds and know that winning streaks run out. They develop strategies to make the odds more in their favor, whether they're playing craps, poker, or blackjack.

If you don't want to gamble away your retirement money, you need a strategy. To handle your investments and keep them growing.

That is your primary objective now—growth. Not income from your investments, but growth so you'll have income when you retire. Your objective should cover all your investment decisions. It means you'll have to make some hard decisions. It means that you'll have to accept some risks. Because otherwise your investments won't grow sufficiently to meet your retirement needs.

How can you tell exactly when to buy and sell? A lot depends on how involved an investor you are or intend to be.

If you're reading the newspaper stock pages every day, subscribing to financial newsletters, and reading a variety of business publications, you can be involved enough to anticipate turning points in the economy or the market. If you see one coming, sell those assets that will be hurt by a change in the economy or market and buy assets that a market or economic shift will bolster. If you're supremely confident, you might switch all your assets from one type of investment to another.

For people without that expertise or degree of active participation, such a course would be like putting all your money on a 50-1 shot at the racetrack.

So what do you do if you find picking a switch in the economic stream as mystifying as women's dress sizes or studying the economy and markets as alluring as tofu?

You could hire a financial planner or a broker to handle and monitor your investments. But that means having a substantial portfolio for them to work with—a minimum of $100,000. Usually, much more. And even then, you have to take an active interest in what they do: Make sure you fully understand their advice.

If you don't have that kind of money to begin with, though, you need to develop an allocation scheme for your investment portfolio that will help you decide when to shift your investments so that you buy low and sell high.

How do you do that?

First, you have to decide how much short-term risk you can afford to take.

For example, if you're 40, you have plenty of time until you retire. So you can afford short-term losses in investment values as long as ultimately (at retirement) those investments give you the most return.

If you're 50, you can't take as much risk. You need a lot of growth but can't afford to wait five or 10 years for a sour economy to turn around.

Then there is psychology.

If you are nervous, you'll want a balanced portfolio that protects against almost all contingencies. You can buy mutual funds, commodity funds, and REITs to do that. There is even a mutual fund that shifts its portfolio of investments to maintain a fifth share each in stocks, bonds, metal stocks, real estate, and certificates of deposit.

If you aren't afraid of economic roller coaster rides, you can afford to invest more in growth-oriented stocks and mutual funds, which have the highest long-term total returns.

In addition to age and psychology, there's how much money you have to start with. Before you invest in anything other than a money market account or rollover CDs, you need to build a cash reserve. That reserve should be enough to carry you through two months. (You can figure the amount from reviewing your budget.) After that you can invest money in quickly marketable blue-chip securities, preferably stocks or stock mutual funds that provide high dividends, until you have enough in cash and securities to last you another four months.

Those investments provide the base for your investment allocation scheme and begin your buy and sell strategy for investing.

Certainly, it's unbalanced. It doesn't include commodities, bonds, or real estate. But because interest rates on CDs and bonds tend to move in the same direction and counter to the stock market, you can use the values in your limited portfolio to tell you when it is a good time to buy other investments.

By putting two months' worth of base income in cash (CDs or money markets) and four months' worth into stocks, you are allocating a third of your investments to cash, which will grow with higher interest in inflationary times, and allocating two-thirds to stocks, which tend to increase with economic growth.

If interest rates rise and returns are reinvested while stock prices fall, your cash account goes up as a percentage of your investments while the value of stocks as a percentage of your investments falls. That's the time to buy growth stocks or put money in long-term bonds, which also might be down in price.

If inflation is low and interest rates are down, stock prices are likely to go up. That unbalances your portfolio in stocks. What you should do then is take your gains in stocks and new savings and put them into REITs or, possibly, a commodity or gold-mining fund that is likely to be down in price. You should also add a little bit to cash, even though it isn't earning very much, because you'll want money there to put in stocks when the economy shifts again.

In that way, you start to diversify and balance your portfolio. As it does so, you'll have to figure the exact mix you want to aim for and maintain over a 10-year period.

IMPLEMENTING AN ASSET ALLOCATION PLAN: AN EXAMPLE

There is no golden formula for a mix. Recommendations vary from 45 percent in bonds, 35 percent in stocks, and 20 percent in cash to 80 percent in stocks, 10 percent in bonds, and 10 percent in cash. That's a broad range.

For someone at age 50, the best allocation would be closer to 30 percent stocks, 25 percent bonds, 20 percent real estate, 10 percent gold or commodities, 15 percent cash. The stocks, though, would be more blue chip—up to half. The reason? Because eventually you'll want to move your money into income-producing investments, and you'll want to time your moves to when you can get the best income-producing buys. Growth stocks are often volatile enough to allow you to do that. And economic turns can last a decade.

Once you've decided the portfolio mix you want to maintain, here's how your allocation plan can help with your investment decisions. I've simplified it by using a 20 percent across-the-board mix of the main investment categories.

In this example, I start with a base of $25,000 and assume a portfolio of stock mutual funds in which dividends are reinvested, bond mutual funds with 8 percent interest which isn't reinvested (although it could be), metals stock funds (also reinvested), real estate REITs with dividends reinvested, and a money market account earning a compounded annual rate of 7 percent. In addition, there's a savings plan that invests $400 into each account in equal monthly increments throughout the year (or 33.33/month/account). As in table 12.1, the example would fit with a 4 percent inflation rate and 3 percent economic growth rate with a forecast of continued growth and slightly higher inflation to come.

TABLE 12.1 Asset Allocation: An Example

Year 1: Scenario
Investment mix: 20 percent
Reinvested dividends: Stocks and metals, mutual funds, REITs
Investment base: $25,000
Bond mutual fund: 8% interest
Money market account: Compounded annual rate, 7%
Savings allocation: $400 per month
Inflation rate: 4%
Economic growth: 3%

	Stocks 50 shares @ $100/sh.	Bonds 50 shares @ $100/sh.	Metals 50 shares @ $100/sh.	Real Estate 5 shares @ $1,000/sh.	Cash $5,000
Year 0:					
Value:	$5,000	$5,000	$5,000	$5,000	same
Year 1:	*Add growth/decline market value.*				
	up $500 +$10/sh.	down $200 -$4/sh.	down $100 -$2/sh.	up $500 +$500/sh.	—
Value:	$5,500	$4,800	$4,900	$5,500	$5,000
	Add dividends and interest.				
	$200	$0	$250	$250	$350
Value after dividends/interest:					
	$5,700	$4,800	$5,150	$5,750	$5,350

Total value old investments = $26,750.

	Add money invested throughout the year.				
	$400	$400	$400	$400	$400
	$6,100	$5,200	$5,550	$6,150	$5,750
	Add growth/decline in new investments.				
	up $15	down $4	down $2	up $16	—
	$6,115	$5,196	$5,548	$6,166	$5,750
	Add dividends/interest from new investments.				
	$7	$0	$9	$9	$7
Value after dividends/interest from new investments:					
	$6,122	$5,196	$5,557	$6,175	$5,757

Value of investments starting year 2 = $28,807.

Portfolio mix:

	21.3%	18.0%	19.3%	21.4%	20%
	sell	buy	buy	sell	buy
	$361	$565	$204	$414	$4
Value at 20% mix:					
	$5,761	$5,761	$5,761	$5,761	$5,761

TABLE 12.1 Asset Allocation: An Example *(Continued)*

Year 2: Scenario
Inflation: 5%, interest rates rising
Economic growth: 3.5%
Note: Your return on bonds increases to 8.3% because
of your purchases and your return on money market jumps to 8%.
Dividends from your stock funds, though, drop to 3.3% because
of rise in price. This year, your savings increase to $4,000.

	Stocks $5,761	Bonds $5,761	Metals $5,761	Real Estate $5,761	Cash $5,761
	Add growth/decline market value.				
Year 2:	up $150	down $250	up $100	up $600	—
	$5,911	$5,511	$5,861	$6,361	$5,761
	Add dividends and interest.				
	$190	$0	$288	$288	$461
	$6,101	$5,511	$6,149	$6,649	$6,222
	Add money invested throughout the year.				
	$800	$800	$800	$800	$800
	$6,901	$6,311	$6,949	$7,449	$7,022
	Add growth/decline in new investments.				
	up $13	down $14	up $12	up $56	—
	$6,914	$6,297	$6,961	$7,505	$7,022
	Add dividends/interest from new investments.				
	$16	$0	$27	$27	$32
	$6,930	$6,297	$6,988	$7,532	$7,054
Portfolio mix:					
	19.9%	18.1%	20.1%	21.6%	20.3%
	buy	buy	sell	sell	sell
	$30	$663	$28	$572	$94
Value at 20% mix:					
	$6,960	$6,960	$6,960	$6,960	$6,960

And so on . . .

At some points stocks will go down, and you'll buy them. At some points real estate will hit the skids, and then you'll buy that. Note that you never just sell out anything. In fact, your holdings are meant to increase in all categories. You take advantage of dollar-cost averaging in your purchases of investments whenever possible, buying them throughout the year, if possible, with your dividends and then averaging the cost year-to-year by maintaining your portfolio allocation formula.

The ultimate aim is to try and increase your shares in any investment category when it costs the least and sell shares when they are relatively high so you can capture some of the gain.

The key, of course, is picking good investments to start with. Do your research early, then let the strategy shift so you aren't out of balance. As you grow older and want to allocate more of your savings in safer, income-producing investments, you simply use your new savings to make those purchases.

Another key that can improve this scheme is to monitor it every month, just to make sure your balance isn't way out of kilter. The stock market runup before Black Monday in October 1987 was steep and fast.

By monitoring your portfolio every month, you would have locked in large amounts of those gains before the fall. And after the crash, you would have been in the market buying shares at discounted levels. You would have bought low and sold high.

But buying low and selling high can help you only if you can keep and reinvest what you get. And Uncle Sam isn't exactly there to help you. In fact, he wants a cut of the action.

So you have to find ways to reduce his take at least while your investments grow. You must run for some tax shelters.

SHELTER YOUR INCOME

Because Uncle Sam doesn't want the rich to grow richer, he taxes savings and investments so that those who are in the middle find it harder to keep from growing poorer as they grow older. He ignores the fact that inflation erodes the value of savings interest and investment income. He barely thinks about the risk you take with investing. And then he decries the fact that Americans buy, buy, buy, as the tax laws encourage.

So you have to finagle as you save by making use of the scant tools Uncle Sam gives you.

One tool is the deductibility of losses from any of your investments. If you buy a stock or bond and then later sell it for less than you paid for it, you have a loss that you can deduct from any gains you earn from other investments. And even if you have no gains, you can deduct up to $3,000 in such losses from ordinary income—that's the money you work for.

Here's how you can use this to your advantage in managing your portfolio.

You've been buying a stock mutual fund through reinvestment of dividends and also been investing in a bond fund with an 8.5 percent annual return at the start of the year.

Here's how it looks (see Table 12.2):

TABLE 12.2 Charting Movements of Your Investments for Tax Sheltering

Transaction	Purchase Date	# Shares Bought	@ Price	Total Value
XYZ Growth	1/1/90	200	@ $100	$20,000
ABC Bond	1/1/90	10	1,000	10,000
ABC Bond	3/15/90	10	990	9,990
XYZ Growth	6/30/90	5	110	550
ABC Bond	9/15/90	0.5	970	485
XYZ Growth	12/30/90	5	110	550
ABC Bond	12/30/90	0.5	970	485
ABC Bond	3/15/91	0.5	950	475
XYZ Growth	6/30/91	4	120	480
ABC Bond	9/15/91	0.5	930	465
XYZ Growth	12/30/91	4	125	500

Summary 1990–91	Total # Shares Bought	Total Paid	Current Value
XYZ Growth	218	$22,080	$125 x 218 = $27,250
ABC Bond	22	21,810	930 x 22 = 20,460

At the end of two years, you want to capture some of the gains that you earned on your stocks, balance your portfolio between stocks and bonds, and buy more bonds at the $930 selling price because the 9.1 percent return looks good.

If the money was in a tax-deferred IRA or a 401(K) plan, all you would have to do would be to divide the $6,790 difference between your stock and bond accounts by selling $3,395 worth of stock and buy $3,395 worth of bonds. That could be nearly accomplished simply by selling 27 shares of the 200 shares you bought on 1/1/90 or $100 a share that are now worth $125 a share, raising $3,375.

But if your money isn't in a tax-deferred account, you wouldn't want to do that. For with tax rates of between 15 percent and 33 percent, depending on your income, the tax on the $675 gain would reduce it by between $90.75 and $222.75, leaving you with that much less to buy bonds. That would be foolish.

So, first of all you want to take the lowest gains possible on your stocks. You do that by first selling the 18 shares you bought on 6/30/90, 12/30/90, 6/30/91, and 12/30/91. That raises $2,250 with gains of only $170. You also sell 9 shares of stock you bought on 1/1/90 for $100 a share that are now worth $125 a share. That raises $1,125 with a $225 gain.

But you still haven't reached the balance you want. To accomplish that, you need to sell all the bonds you bought for $1,000 that now sell for $930. That raises $9,300 and results in a $700 loss.

You now have $12,675 in cash ($2,250 + $1,125 + $9,300) that you can pump into buying new bonds at $930 each, effectively balancing your bond and stock portfolio. But you don't pay any taxes. In fact, you can deduct a net capital loss of $305 (gains of $170 + $225 from the sale of stocks – the loss of $700 from the sale of bonds. That amounts to a savings to you of $45 to $100 on taxes—or a third to a half share of stock.

The key is that whenever you take a gain on any stock or bond or other investment, look for investments that you bought high and take losses on them at the same time.

If you're going to sell investments to take gains rather than hold them long-term, don't just hold on to losing investments hoping they'll eventually regain value. If you have that much faith in them, sell off your losses and reinvest at the lower price taking advantage of the tax deductions you can get. By applying the tax savings—between $450 and $1,000 on a $3000 loss—to buying new shares, you can increase your shares and reap bigger gains later.

For example, you bought 1,000 shares of High Growth at $30 a share. Its price drops to $27 a share. You think it will rebound with the economy, so you hold on and it does—jumping to $36 a share. When you sell it and then pay 28 percent in taxes on your gain—$1,680—your profit is $4,320. Pat yourself on the back.

But what would have happened if you sold at $27 and then bought back in? Sell at $27,000 and take a loss of $3,000 and you can count on an $840 reduction in your taxes.

If you use a discount broker, your fees for such transactions should be less than $250. Because that is also deductible and is less than your tax savings, you make more by selling and repurchasing than by simply holding on while the stock is down.

Taking losses isn't the only way to shelter money.

Remember, from the earlier section on pensions, that defined contribution plans, 401(K) plans, and profit-sharing plans can be used to shelter your savings from taxes. In addition, there is the individual retirement account.

Tax reform took away deductibility of IRA contributions for many tax-payers. But you can still take the full $2,000 deduction for an IRA if you aren't covered by a company pension plan, profit-sharing plan, an ESOP, a 401(K) plan, a SEP, or a federal, state, or other government employee pension plan no matter what your income is.

If either spouse is covered by a plan, he or she is treated as if both are covered unless they file separate tax returns. Still you can also make the full deduction for an IRA if your joint adjusted gross income is less than $40,000. And single taxpayers can fully deduct their IRA contribution if their adjusted gross income is less than $25,000.

For each $1,000 of income above those levels, you can deduct $200 less for an IRA contribution—down to a $200 deduction at $50,000 on a joint return and $35,000 on a single return.

For married couples below the limit with both working, each can take a full $2,000 deduction. With one spouse not working, they can take an added $250 IRA deduction by opening a second account for the non-working spouse. You just can't contribute more than $2,000 to a single account.

If you are in an income bracket that won't allow an IRA deduction, it still can be worth putting money into one because the interest, dividends, and capital gains it earns aren't taxed—at the federal, state, and local level—until the money is withdrawn.

That can mean the difference between your investments compounding at a rate of 10 percent versus compounding at 6 percent, which can make a big difference over 20 years.

The one thing you have to remember about an IRA is that you can't withdraw before reaching age 59½ without paying a 10 percent penalty in addition to regular taxes.

The best use of an IRA under an allocation plan is to buy investments for an IRA account only when the scheme tells you they are relatively low in price, using new savings for the purchases.

Later, you should sell investments in the IRA only when they produce a gain, unless they've turned in to a real dog, because you can't deduct losses in IRA accounts from your income.

Annuities that you can purchase through an insurance company provide another tax-exempt way of compounding. But the returns on annuities aren't as good as for most other investments.

Finally, you can shelter your income from taxes by investing in tax-free municipal bonds or tax-free municipal bond funds.

Table 12.3 shows what tax-free yields are worth at various tax rates.

As these yields show, tax-free municipal bonds make a lot more sense the higher your tax bracket. But even then, you don't want to be totally invested in tax-frees. You never know exactly what the economy is going to do.

That's the reason that you need to diversify your investments. If inflation beats your after tax yield on any investment, you lose. And you can't afford to lose across the board. If you diversify your investments, you won't. If you

Table 12.3 Real Values of Tax-Free Investment Yields

	Taxable Yield at		
Tax-Free Yield	15%	28%	33%
5%	5.9%	6.9%	7.5%
5.5	6.5	7.6	8.2
6	7.1	8.3	9
6.5	7.7	9	9.7
7	8.2	9.7	10.5
7.5	8.8	10.4	11.2
8	9.4	11.1	11.9
8.5	10.0	11.8	12.7

diversify your investments, you'll increase your chances of maximizing your growth without gambling with your savings and your retirement.

Just remember:

Don't panic.

Buy low, sell high.

Shelter some of your income.

And get good financial advice and keep good records.

Which is what our next Chapter is about.

13

Handling Retirement, or For the Record

So, now you're all hyped up to start investing and make your money grow. Yeah, I know. Investing can be nerve-wracking, with all the choices that are available. That's why you wade in slowly.

A money market account first. Then CDs in a rollover account. Then mutual funds.

With such investments, you begin to get a feel for investment jargon and for investing. Just don't be afraid to make some choices. Because you aren't going to invest all your money in any one investment—and because mutual funds are diversified anyway—you won't lose everything. The only way you really lose is by not investing at all. Then your money never grows, and you never save enough to retire comfortably.

So pick a few things and get started.

As I said earlier, you can start at your bank with cash accounts, CDs, and an IRA.

Through magazines and books such as *The Individual Investor's Guide to No Load Mutual Funds*, you can start investing in mutual funds. You contact each fund directly for prospectuses, then choose two or three to get started.

RECORDKEEPING IS ESSENTIAL AND FUN

But you still have the responsibility to watch over your little nest egg and nurture it. And for that you have to keep records.

More fun! Well, sort of.

If you could just think of your records as baseball statistics or keeping tabs on a movie idol, then it would be fun. Imagine it as counting money. Most people like to do that. Watch Monopoly® players. They're always counting their money, totaling up their assets, determining whether they have enough to buy houses and hotels.

Recordkeeping is like setting up your properties in a Monopoly® game. No different. It's just that you have to make the cards up rather than having them given to you in the pack.

Oh, sure, I know that monopoly is a game, and your investments are real life. But if you treat investing more as a game than as a necessity, you might enjoy it more and do better at it. And treating your records as a tool for keeping score rather than as a mundane chore can make it more interesting and enjoyable.

And since you need to keep tabs on your records you might as well enjoy them. That's one reason why I'll give you only samples on how to keep score. You don't have to absolutely follow my method. If you can find some way to make your recordkeeping more interesting, go for it.

These, though, are the basic rules for recordkeeping:

- Keep it simple.

- Make it complete.

- Separate the vital from the curious.

- Summarize.

Now those are pretty simple rules. But the overriding rule is: Know what your records are for. There are three reasons to keep records:

- To know what you have.

- To evaluate your performance.

- To have a record for Uncle Sam.

Here's what each of those involve:

- To know what you have

    — Name of firm.
    — Type of investment (stock, mutual fund, bond, REIT, etc.).
    — Number of shares.
    — Current value of investment.
    — Dates when dividends, interest, or rents are due.
    — Amount of dividends, interest, or rent.
    — Debts owed on investment (such as the mortgage for a rental property).
    — Your rights in the investment—voting rights as a shareholder, rights in case of bankruptcy, rights as a landlord.
    — Legal obligations, if any, as a result of the investment.

All of those things are pretty self-explanatory. You may wonder, though, why I didn't mention what you paid for your investment. That's simply because what you paid doesn't mean anything as far as what you have. An investment can go down in price or up in price or stay the same. It's worth only what it can sell for. So knowing what you paid for it doesn't mean anything in terms of knowing what you have. You need to know what you paid for it only so you can evaluate your performance and for tax purposes.

- Evaluating your investment.

    — Current value of your investment.
    — Cost of your investment.
    — Current price of your investment per share or unit.
    — Cost of your investment per share or unit.
    — Dividend, interest, or rent from investment.
    — Charges associated with investment (fees and commissions, mortgage interest, income taxes, property taxes, etc.).
    — Period investment has been held.

From those basic facts, you can derive how much your investment is earning—its yield—both in terms of income and increased value (capital gain). And with those factors being taken into account for all of your investments, you can compare them to other potential investments. But you also need:

- Tax records.

    — Date of purchase.
    — Cost at purchase.
    — Share numbers or unit numbers.
    — Records of transaction.
    — Date of sale.
    — Total sale's price.
    — Interest, dividends, rent for tax year.
    — Investment costs, including fees, commissions, property taxes, mortgage interest for rental property.

As you may have noticed, some of the items on the lists duplicate one another. That's why you can combine the forms to suit your particular needs. In fact, you could just lump everything together without any forms—just bits and pieces of papers that you could then drag out and read through when you want to buy or sell an investment or when you have to do your taxes. One giant drawer filled with stuff, though, isn't a very easy way to keep track of anything. It would sort of look like my desk. And I know some things on my desk will never see the light of day ever again—like the top of it.

There is a better way, though, that will save you time and effort and agonizing: Keep a separate set of files for your investments in a separate box. And keep an investment book.

I suggest a separate box because then you won't have to wade through the household bills to find the prospectus for your mutual fund. Furthermore, a fireproof box for your investment papers can save you a lot of worry.

Things I would not keep with my investments are: The actual certificates of ownership—deeds, warrants, stocks, bonds. Those should go in a safety deposit box at a bank, where they are absolutely safe from loss or theft. It's a pain to try to get stock reissued or to get a new copy of a contract. You can keep copies of those things at home, but the originals along with your will and the family jewels should be put in a safety deposit box at the bank with one or two other people you trust having a key and access to them.

What do you keep in your files, then? The most recent prospectus for each investment. The transaction slips for each investment. The earnings reports or account statements. That's it. You keep one file for each investment. You can put them in alphabetical order or order your files in investment groups—cash accounts, stocks and bonds, real estate, commodities and collectibles. One or two extra files can keep clips on potential investments, including any research you do on particular companies or stocks.

Keep statements in order by date and use a *large* paperclip to hold them together; staple your transaction slips to the inside edges of your folder; keep the prospectus at the rear of the file.

Believe it or not, such orderly handling of your files can help make you more decisive about your investments. Investing is a matter of attitude—playact as if you are an investor and you will *be* an investor (Zen economics 101). Just make sure you use *real* money when you go to your broker to buy something.

Keeping an investment book also is part of the game. It makes things concrete that often seem unreal.

I suggest a looseleaf notebook so that you can add pages and take out pages easily. You can keep just a record of your investments or include information on insurance and taxes. You can buy a notebook at an office supply shop or put one together yourself.

At the front of the notebook, keep a tickler file with dates when dividends and interest are due.

My tickler looks like Table 13.1.

This tickler chart lets me know my investment cash flow. If I don't get a check when it should arrive, I can contact my broker or the company that I've invested in and ask what happened. I'll know quickly if something has gone

TABLE 13.1 Tickler Chart

Investment	Jan	Feb	Mar	Apr	May	June	July	Aug	Sep	Oct	Nov	Dec
1. day	—	—	—	—	—	—	—	—	—	—	—	—
amount	—	—	—	—	—	—	—	—	—	—	—	—
2. day	—	—	—	—	—	—	—	—	—	—	—	—
amount	—	—	—	—	—	—	—	—	—	—	—	—
3. day	—	—	—	—	—	—	—	—	—	—	—	—
amount	—	—	—	—	—	—	—	—	—	—	—	—
4. day	—	—	—	—	—	—	—	—	—	—	—	—
amount	—	—	—	—	—	—	—	—	—	—	—	—
5. day	—	—	—	—	—	—	—	—	—	—	—	—
amount	—	—	—	—	—	—	—	—	—	—	—	—
6. day	—	—	—	—	—	—	—	—	—	—	—	—
amount	—	—	—	—	—	—	—	—	—	—	—	—
7. day	—	—	—	—	—	—	—	—	—	—	—	—
amount	—	—	—	—	—	—	—	—	—	—	—	—
8. day	—	—	—	—	—	—	—	—	—	—	—	—
amount	—	—	—	—	—	—	—	—	—	—	—	—
9. day	—	—	—	—	—	—	—	—	—	—	—	—
amount	—	—	—	—	—	—	—	—	—	—	—	—
10. day	—	—	—	—	—	—	—	—	—	—	—	—
amount	—	—	—	—	—	—	—	—	—	—	—	—
Totals	=	=	=	=	=	=	=	=	=	=	=	=

wrong and can anticipate making new investments with my proceeds. The tickler is especially useful for keeping tabs on CDs in rollover accounts. It is a simple calendar that gears you for action.

INVESTMENT EVALUATION

My investment evaluation report, Figure 13.1, is a bit more complicated. This form lets you quickly compare how your individual investments are doing and

FIGURE 13.1 Investment Returns
Part I

Date: (fill in when evaluation was made): _____
Period of Evaluation: _____

Type	Shares Units[a] Amount	Original Cost[b] Amount	Market Price		Capital Gains	
			Start[c] Amount	End[d] Amount	Realized[e] Amount	Unrealized[f] Amount
Stocks						
Mutual Fund						
1.	____	____	____	____	____	____
2.	____	____	____	____	____	____
3.	____	____	____	____	____	____
4.	____	____	____	____	____	____
5.	____	____	____	____	____	____
Stock						
1.	____	____	____	____	____	____
2.	____	____	____	____	____	____
3.	____	____	____	____	____	____
4.	____	____	____	____	____	____
5.	____	____	____	____	____	____
Bonds						
Income Fund						
1.	____	____	____	____	____	____
2.	____	____	____	____	____	____
3.	____	____	____	____	____	____
4.	____	____	____	____	____	____
5.	____	____	____	____	____	____
Bond						
1.	____	____	____	____	____	____
2.	____	____	____	____	____	____
3.	____	____	____	____	____	____
4.	____	____	____	____	____	____
5.	____	____	____	____	____	____
Subtotal	____	____	____	____	____	____
Money						
CDs						
1.	____	____	____	____	____	____
2.	____	____	____	____	____	____
3.	____	____	____	____	____	____
4.	____	____	____	____	____	____
5.	____	____	____	____	____	____

Continued

Type	Shares Units[a] Amount	Original Cost[b] Amount	Market Price		Capital Gains	
			Start[c] Amount	End[d] Amount	Realized[e] Amount	Unrealized[f] Amount
T-notes						
1.	____	____	____	____	____	____
2.	____	____	____	____	____	____
3.	____	____	____	____	____	____
4.	____	____	____	____	____	____
5.	____	____	____	____	____	____
Money Mkt.						
1.	____	____	____	____	____	____
2.	____	____	____	____	____	____
3.	____	____	____	____	____	____
4.	____	____	____	____	____	____
5.	____	____	____	____	____	____
Subtotal	____	____	____	____	____	____
Commodities						
1.	____	____	____	____	____	____
2.	____	____	____	____	____	____
3.	____	____	____	____	____	____
4.	____	____	____	____	____	____
5.	____	____	____	____	____	____
Subtotal	____	____	____	____	____	____
Real Estate						
REITs	____	____	____	____	____	____
Unit Trust	____	____	____	____	____	____
Ltd. Partner	____	____	____	____	____	____
Rentals	____	____	____	____	____	____
	____	____	____	____	____	____
	____	____	____	____	____	____
Subtotal	____	____	____	____	____	____
TOTAL	====	====	====	====	====	====

Total Invested: $_____   Percent Invested: Stocks _____%
                                                 Bonds _____%
                                                 Money _____%
                                          Commodities _____%
                                          Real Estate _____%

[a] Number of shares or units of investment. For limited partnerships or rental properties, 1 for each owned.

[b] What you paid for the investment.

[c] Value of investment at start of evaluation period.

[d] Value of investment at end of evaluation period.

[e] Capital gain if investment was reinvested—mutual fund.

[f] Capital gain at end of period for unsold asset.

FIGURE 13.1 Investment Returns
Part II

Date: (fill in when evaluation was made): _____
Period of Evaluation: _____

Type	Dividends Interest[g] Amount	Fees/ Costs[h] Amount	Estimate of Taxes[i] Amount	Net Return[j] Amount	True Yield[k] Amount
Stocks					
Mutual Fund					
1.	_____	_____	_____	_____	_____
2.	_____	_____	_____	_____	_____
3.	_____	_____	_____	_____	_____
4.	_____	_____	_____	_____	_____
5.	_____	_____	_____	_____	_____
Stock					
1.	_____	_____	_____	_____	_____
2.	_____	_____	_____	_____	_____
3.	_____	_____	_____	_____	_____
4.	_____	_____	_____	_____	_____
5.	_____	_____	_____	_____	_____
Bonds					
Income Fund					
1.	_____	_____	_____	_____	_____
2.	_____	_____	_____	_____	_____
3.	_____	_____	_____	_____	_____
4.	_____	_____	_____	_____	_____
5.	_____	_____	_____	_____	_____
Bond					
1.	_____	_____	_____	_____	_____
2.	_____	_____	_____	_____	_____
3.	_____	_____	_____	_____	_____
4.	_____	_____	_____	_____	_____
5.	_____	_____	_____	_____	_____
Subtotal	_____	_____	_____	_____	_____
Money					
CDs					
1.	_____	_____	_____	_____	_____
2.	_____	_____	_____	_____	_____
3.	_____	_____	_____	_____	_____
4.	_____	_____	_____	_____	_____
5.	_____	_____	_____	_____	_____

Continued

Type	Dividends Interest[g] Amount	Fees/ Costs[h] Amount	Estimate of Taxes[i] Amount	Net Return[j] Amount	True Yield[k] Amount
T-notes					
1.	____	____	____	____	____
2.	____	____	____	____	____
3.	____	____	____	____	____
4.	____	____	____	____	____
5.	____	____	____	____	____
Money Mkt.					
1.	____	____	____	____	____
2.	____	____	____	____	____
3.	____	____	____	____	____
4.	____	____	____	____	____
5.	____	____	____	____	____
Subtotal	____	____	____	____	____
Commodities					
1.	____	____	____	____	____
2.	____	____	____	____	____
3.	____	____	____	____	____
4.	____	____	____	____	____
5.	____	____	____	____	____
Subtotal	____	____	____	____	____
Real Estate					
REITs	____	____	____	____	____
Unit Trust	____	____	____	____	____
Ltd. Partner	____	____	____	____	____
Rentals	____	____	____	____	____
	____	____	____	____	____
	____	____	____	____	____
Subtotal	____	____	____	____	____
TOTAL	====	====	====	====	====

Total Invested: $_____

Percent Invested: Stocks ____%
Bonds ____%
Money ____%
Commodities ____%
Real Estate ____%

[g] Income from investment, including dividends, interest, rents.

[h] Commissions, administration fees; for rental property, maintenance, depreciation, property taxes, mortgage.

[i] Income taxes, your federal rate plus state rate. Multiply by [e] or [f] plus [g] minus [h].

[j] Net return for period being evaluated equals [e] or [f] plus [g] minus [h] minus [i].

[k] True Yield. [j] divided by [c] equals your yield for the period. To get yearly rate of yield if done quarterly, multiply by 4; semiannually, multiply by 2.

how your investments are piling up in different categories to meet your diversification goals.

To make this form usable you have to follow some simple rules:

1. Don't use it to evaluate investments you've already sold.

   Things you've sold don't need to be evaluated. You've already evaluated them and your decision was to sell them. Investments still in your possession await a decision. That's what you need to evaluate.

   So don't try to summarize on this form how well a past investment performed. In addition to not helping you make a future decision, it tremendously complicates the calculations you need to develop a yield. For exmple, how are you going to figure out the true yield for investments you still hold from a batch of 200 shares of XYZ Corp., if you include 50 shares sold at a 20 percent gain 63 days into the year? And why would you want to know that? After all, you can't sell those same shares again.

2. Evaluate separately the investments bought throughout your evaluation period—even if they are issues of stocks and bonds for the same company for which you already hold stocks and bonds or are in the same mutual fund, or REIT, or other investment.

   The reason, again, is to make calculating the returns on your investments, their yields, as simple as possible.

   It is very easy to figure out the total true yield (y) of dividends and growth from an investment you've held through a full year or evaluation period. It's simply the market value at the end of the period (p1) minus the market value at the beginning of the period (p) plus dividends (d) divided by the market value at the start of the period (p), the result of which is multiplied by 100 (to convert to a percentage). If the period is less than a year, divide 365 by the number of days in the period and then multiply the percentage by the resulting product to get an annual yield. The formula is:

$$[(p1 - p) + d] + p \times 100 = y$$

   Slugging numbers in, the market value of 200 shares of XYZ Corp. at the start of the year was $2,000, or $10 a share for 200 shares, a figure you checked at the start of the year from the stock lists in your newspaper. The market value at the end of the year for the 200 shares was $2,400, or $12 a share. You were paid $25, or 12.5 cents a share, for each quarter. That's $100 in dividends for the year.

   Your total yield would be what? Try to figure it out before looking at the answer on page 125.

Did you come up with 25 percent?
Here's the math:

$$\$2{,}400 \ (p1) - 2{,}000 \ (p) = \$400$$

$$\$400 + \$100 \ (d) = \$500$$

$$\$500 \div \$2{,}000 \ (p) = 0.25$$

$$0.25 \times 100 = 25 \text{ percent } (y)$$

You might wonder why gains and dividends are divided by the market value at the start of the period rather than the amount actually paid for the investment, the original cost also on the form, or by the market value at the end of the year.

The answer is that you're evaluating the period for which the investment report was written. By keeping investment reports from year to year, you keep track of how your investments are doing over time. And you should keep each evaluation report and compare the figures—even charting the annual yields of your investments to see how they compare over a series of evaluation periods.

But for the period under evaluation, it doesn't matter if your investment was worth $8 or $8,000 three years ago. What matters is its worth at the start of the period and the end of the period. And because the start of the period is your base for evaluating the stock, bond, or mutual fund, you divide by the value at the start of the period value (p) so you know how much you've gained from that point.

EVALUATION BY DOLLAR-COST AVERAGING

But what about the purchases you make of a specific investment throughout a period? Well, you can try to figure out the yield of stocks you've held the whole period and those you bought each month at different prices. It can be done, but it complicates your calculations and takes away an analytical tool. Those shares bought throughout the period can give you a clue on how your stock is moving— whether it is increasing steadily or whether it increased heavily at the beginning or end of the period. Using Table 13.2 you can account for investments bought throughout the year by dollar-cost averaging.

It's easy to see the original cost of your investment here. It's the $600 you paid for the shares. That also is an average market price for what you could call the start of the year. The market value at the end of the year is equal to the number of shares (55.59) times the market price at the end of the year ($12), $667.08. So, what is the total yield?

TABLE 13.2 Accounting for Your Investments

Purchase Date	Amount Invested	No. of Shares Purchased	Price per Share	Total Shares	Dividend
1/15	$50	5	$10	5	
2/15	50	4.878	10.25	9.878	
3/15	50	4.878	10.25	14.756	$1.84
4/15	50	5	10	19.756	
5/15	50	4.762	10.50	24.518	
6/15	50	4.651	10.75	29.169	3.65
7/15	50	4.651	10.75	33.820	
8/15	50	4.556	11	38.376	
9/15	50	4.444	11.25	42.82	5.35
10/15	50	4.348	11.5	47.168	
11/15	50	4.255	11.75	51.423	
12/15	50	4.167	12	55.29	6.95
Total	$600	55.59	—	55.59	$17.79

Well, p1 = $667.08, p = $600, d = $17.79, so:

$$667.08 - \$600 = \$67.08$$

$$67.08 + \$17.79 = \$84.87$$

$$84.87 + \$600 = 0.141$$

$$0.141 \times 100 = 14.1\%$$

But is 14.1 percent a true picture of the yield earned from the new shares? Not really. It is an average yield, "pretending" that each month's investment actually had 12 months to grow. That isn't true. So, what is a true picture of the yield? In this example, it's simple. The average time held for all of the new purchases is six months. That's half a year. True yield of these purchases over a full year is double that of a half year. So, you merely multiply the yield from this dollar-cost averaging of stock by two. That gives you a yield of 28.2 percent.

What does that tell you when you compare it to the 25 percent yield from shares you held over a full year? (Remember the formula: $60 value at end of year – $50 value when purchased = $10 + $2.50 worth of dividends at 12.5 cents per quarter per share = $12.50 + $50 = 0.25 x 100 = 25 percent). It tells you that prices for stocks increased most at the end of the year. If they had increased most early in the year, then you would have been able to buy fewer shares. Fewer shares would mean a lower market value at the end of the year and lower dividends. Your yield on your new purchases would then have been less than for the investments you held for the full year.

If you purchase investments haphazardly throughout the year, though, this analytical tool doesn't work because some investments will be weighted improperly. See Table 13.3 for an example:

TABLE 13.3 Accounting for Haphazard Investments

Purchase Date	Amount Invested	No. of Shares Purchased	Price per Share	Total Shares	Dividend
5/15	$300	28.570	$10.50	28.57	
6/15	—	—	—	—	$3.57
8/15	200	18.224	11.00	46.794	
9/15	—	—	—	—	5.85
11/15	100	8.511	—	55.305	
12/15	—	—	—	—	6.91
Total	**$600**	55.305	—	—	**$16.33**

What's the yield? Go to the formula: p1 = $649.83, p = $600, d = $16.33. Yield will equal = $66.16 + $600 = 0.11 x 100 = 11%. But that's not a true yield for these investments for a full 12 months. You have to convert each purchase to an annual yield by multiplying each by the 365 days of the year and then dividing it by the number of days each was held. Here's how that works out:

For stocks purchased on 5/15, p1 = $342.84, p = $300, d = $10.71, t (time held) = 230. So, $342.84 – $300 = 42.84 + $10.71 = $53.55 + $300 = 0.178 x 100 = 17.8% x 365 = 6,497 + 230 = 28.2%.

For stocks purchased on 8/15, p1 = $218.69, p = $200, d = $4.56, t = 138. So, $218.69 – $200 = $18.69 + $4.56 = $23.25 + 200 = 0.116 x 100 = 11.6% x 365 = 4234 + 138 = 30.7%

For stocks purchased on 11/15, p1 = $102.13, p = $100, d = $1.06, t = 46. So, $102.13 – 100 = $2.13 + $1.06 = $3.19 – 100 = 0.032 x 100 = 3.2% x 365 = 1,168 – 46 = 25.4%.

Now, that you have each of the annual yields for each of the purchases, what is the average yield for all them? To get that you have to weight each investment by the amount purchased. You paid three times as much on 5/15 as on 11/15, twice as much on 8/15 as 11/15. So, (28.2% x 3) + (30.7% x 2) + 25.4% = 171.4 – 6 (3 + 2 + 1) = 28.6%.

You might think that's crazy because even though you paid the same amount of money as in Table 13.2, you bought fewer shares and received fewer dividends in Table 13.3. So, why a higher total yield? Simple, you held the investments a shorter period of time, and your purchases were all close to the receipt of dividends.

But the point of the exercise is that yield figures from haphazard purchases aren't a good tool for evaluating trends. Averages from regular purchases are.

If you see yields from those kinds of purchases differing from yields of shares you've held throughout the year, it should prompt you to look for reasons why. If the market value flattens out at the end of the year, you must ask if the investment may be reaching the end of its growth. If it increases in value at the end of the year, is it just following the market—in which case you might want to sell some shares—or are its earnings improving enough to make it a hot property—in which case you'd want to hold on and maybe even buy more?

That's the usefulness of keeping this kind of evaluation form. It should prompt you to ask some questions to decide when to sell or buy investments. It should help you control your investments rather than let your investments run on autopilot.

The form also is meant to let you compare different kinds of investments.

But to do that fairly, you have to take into account more than just gains and losses and dividends. You need to account for costs, such as fees, commissions, and maintenance costs, and you need to account for taxes. For example, the yield of a tax-free bond will look a heck of a lot worse than a non-tax-free bond or stock if taxes aren't taken into account.

As you can see, the form in Figure 13.1 includes spaces for those costs and for taxes. Using them you can determine not merely the total yield from an investment but its true, after-tax yield.

This process works by an extension of the preceding yield formula. The added elements are: c for costs, fees, and commissions; t for taxes. Thus:

$$\frac{[\,(p1\text{-}p) + d - c - t\,] \times 100}{p}$$

Again, the start-of-year market value for your shares is $2,000; the end-of-year value is $2,400; the dividends amount to $100. That means you've gotten a total return of $500 this year. But now we throw in an administration fee, like some mutual funds have (in this case $25):

$$\$500 - \$25 = \$475$$

But what about your taxes? Well, they are equal to the total of your local, state, and federal income tax rates. Let's pretend here that the federal rate is 28 percent and that the state rate is 5 percent and that I don't have a city income tax. Together, those rates equal 33 percent, or 0.33 when it is divided by 100. I can estimate my income taxes by:

$$\$475 \times 0.33 = \$156.75$$

Then,

$$\$475 - \$156.75 = \$318.25$$

$$= 0.159 \times 100 = 15.91\%$$

$$\$318.25 + \$2,000 = 0.159 \times 100 = 15.91\%$$

My true after-tax yield is thus 15.91 percent.

There is a simpler method of calculation, though. Simply go like this:

$$\frac{(\$2,400 - \$2,000 + \$100 - \$25) \times (1 - 0.33)}{\$2,000} \times 100 = 15.91\%$$

That's the simple way to find your after tax yield. And you can do that for all your investments to put them on the same level.

KEEP RECORDS FOR *EACH* INVESTMENT

But as important as evaluation is, keeping individual and separate records on each of your investments is also vital. Following here are some examples.

Cash accounts include money market accounts, certificates of deposit, and treasury notes. Table 13.4 shows one way to record them.

Continued on page 132.

TABLE 13.4 Cash Account Records

Investment—Name: _____

Purchase Date/Amount	Int. Rate	Date Due	Int. Rec.	Running Tax	CompAmt	Total Int-Tax	Yield
$1,000	8%	60 days	13.15%	$4.34	$164.38	$8.78	5.3%
——	——	——	——	——	——	——	——
——	——	——	——	——	——	——	——
——	——	——	——	——	——	——	——
——	——	——	——	——	——	——	——

TABLE 13.5 Stock (or Bond) Records—Two Alternatives

Alternative A

Investment, Stock (or Bond): _____

Type: _____   Purpose: _____

Date	No. of Shares Bought	(Sold)	Balance	Share Nos. Bought	(Sold)	Fees Coms.	Cost Bought	(Sold)	Balance
____	____	____	____	____	____	____	____	____	____
____	____	____	____	____	____	____	____	____	____
____	____	____	____	____	____	____	____	____	____
____	____	____	____	____	____	____	____	____	____
____	____	____	____	____	____	____	____	____	____
____	____	____	____	____	____	____	____	____	____
____	____	____	____	____	____	____	____	____	____
____	____	____	____	____	____	____	____	____	____
____	____	____	____	____	____	____	____	____	____
____	____	____	____	____	____	____	____	____	____

Alternative B

Investment, Stock (or Bond): _____

Type: _____   Purpose: _____

Date	No. of Shares Bought (Sold)	Balance	Share Nos. Bought (Sold)	Balance	Fees Coms.
____	____	____	____	____	____
____	____	____	____	____	____
____	____	____	____	____	____
____	____	____	____	____	____
____	____	____	____	____	____
____	____	____	____	____	____
____	____	____	____	____	____
____	____	____	____	____	____
____	____	____	____	____	____
____	____	____	____	____	____

TABLE 13.5 Stock (or Bond) Records—Two Alternatives

Alternative A *(Continued)*

| Price per Unit | | Sales | | | | | Acquiring (Selling) |
Bought	(Sold)	Profit	(Loss)	Date	No. of Shares	Dividends	Agent
——	——	——	——	——	——	——	——
——	——	——	——	——	——	——	——
——	——	——	——	——	——	——	——
——	——	——	——	——	——	——	——
——	——	——	——	——	——	——	——
——	——	——	——	——	——	——	——
——	——	——	——	——	——	——	——
——	——	——	——	——	——	——	——
——	——	——	——	——	——	——	——
——	——	——	——	——	——	——	——

Alternative B *(Continued)*

Cost Bought (Sold)	Balance	Price per Unit Bought (Sold)	Sales Profit (Loss)	No. of Shares	Dividends	Acquiring (Selling) Agent
——	——	——	——	——	——	——
——	——	——	——	——	——	——
——	——	——	——	——	——	——
——	——	——	——	——	——	——
——	——	——	——	——	——	——
——	——	——	——	——	——	——
——	——	——	——	——	——	——
——	——	——	——	——	——	——
——	——	——	——	——	——	——
——	——	——	——	——	——	——

To get a true picture of your real gain, I suggest subtracting an estimate of taxes from the interest you earn. But you also need to be careful not to count the principal amount invested in a rollover CD more than once. That's the reason for the CompAmt category. It means Computed Amount. It is the amount invested times the number of days invested divided by 365.

For example, if you have a $1,000 60-day CD, your computed amount would be $1,000 x 60 = $60,000 divided by 365 = $164.38.

From that you can determine your true yield by subtracting the estimated taxes from the interest earned and then dividing that by CompAmt. For example, if your 60-day earned 8 percent annually, it would give you $13.15 ($164.38 x 0.08). With 28 percent federal and 5 percent state taxes, the estimated tax would be $4.34. Interest minus taxes would be $8.78, and the after-tax yield would be $8.78 divided by $164.38 x 100 (to convert it to a percentage) = 5.3 percent.

That may sound like a lot of computing, but once you start doing it, it becomes automatic. It's really not much different than computing a pitcher's earned-run average, which amounts to Runs Scored – Unearned Runs x 9 (to put them into a base of nine, the number of innings in a game) divided by the actual number of innings. I went to heaven when I was a kid and figured out how ERA was computed. Your true yield is like a pitcher's earned run average—it knocks out the earnings that Uncle Sam taxes away just as the ERA knocks out the runs a pitcher's fielders gave away.

By adding each successive CompAmt and each successive Int-Tax, you get a running true yield that lets you know how your CDs are faring.

The same technique can be applied to Treasury bills and we'll also put it to use in the next category of investing, stocks and bonds. Table 13.5 on pages 130 and 131 provides two alternatives.

This is the B-S method, not for bonds and stocks (or something else). B-S here means Bought and Sold. Put anything that you sell in parentheses (name) on the form; that means you eliminate them. Do the same with losses. But just as you reduce your gain on an investment by the taxes you pay to determine your true yield, you also reduce your losses by the taxes you avoid to determine their exact effect on your finances.

You should include share numbers in your records so that when you sell shares or units you can tell your broker or mutual fund exactly which ones you want to get rid of. By selling shares you bought at the highest price, you reduce your capital gain—but you also cut your capital gains taxes. That's because the IRS follows what is called a First-In, First-Out (FIFO) method of accounting for your investments. If you don't use share numbers and report them at tax time, the IRS will assume you sold the shares you bought first. And since often those shares have the biggest capital gains, you will pay the highest capital gains tax.

Keeping good records not only helps you evaluate and track your investments, it helps you increase your wealth without being penalized by Uncle Sam.

Other sections in your investment book should include real estate and commodities and collectibles.

For REITs, commodity funds, and commodity stocks, use a form exactly like the one for stocks and bonds.

Tables 13.6, 13.7, and 13.8 provide forms for limited partnerships, rental properties, and commodity purchases and collectibles (such as old stamps and artwork).

Table 13.6 Limited Partnerships Record

Name: _____ Acquired through: _____

Date of purchase: _____ Amount of investment: _____ Length: _____

Date	Receipt	Deductions	Est. Taxes	Net Return	Yield
____	____	____	____	____	____
____	____	____	____	____	____
____	____	____	____	____	____
____	____	____	____	____	____
____	____	____	____	____	____

TABLE 13.7 Rental Property Record

Property address: _____ Date of purchase: _____

Price at purchase: _____ Down payment: _____ Closing: _____

Mortgage amount: _____ Rate: _____ Monthly payment: _____

Mortgage Co.: _____ Rental manager: _____

Date	Rents Received	Mortgage Payment	Maint.	Other	Taxes	Yield
____	____	____	____	____	____	____
____	____	____	____	____	____	____
____	____	____	____	____	____	____
____	____	____	____	____	____	____
____	____	____	____	____	____	____

TABLE 13.8 Commodities and Collectibles Record

Commodity or collectibles—name: _____

Purchased from: _____   Price: _____

Appraised by: _____

Date of appraisal: _____   Value at appraisal: _____

You may also want to have a section for insurance in your book. For each insurance policy you have, simply list the name of the company, the agent, the type of insurance, who or what it covers, the cash or surrender value if it is whole life insurance, the amount of coverage, and numbers to call to make claims.

Finally, you can use your book to keep your budget, draw up your net worth, and track your taxes—anything that will make your recordkeeping easier.

And that is about all you really need to start investing and get your retirement nest egg growing. Simple, isn't it?

14

Conclusion, or Facing the Final Curtain

All good things must come to an end. A book. A career. And a life.

When will you die? The answer is simple: When you die. No sooner. No later. You don't know when.

So, there is no sense worrying about when you're going to die. But you should know what you are leaving behind. And to whom.

And that's worth worrying about. You should be a little scared about what happens to those you love after you die. If you don't tie up the loose ends, they'll have to do it without you. And it can tie your family into knots or break it apart.

That's why you need life insurance, as I outlined in Chapter 4. Life insurance passes directly to your spouse or your kids if you die, without having to go through the courts—be probated. It will handle the expenses of your death and provide your spouse and children the money they will need to put their lives back together.

But insurance alone isn't the only thing you need to keep up to date. You need a will and an estate plan that will make it easier for your family after you die, to make it easy for them to go through the necessary grieving process after your death without being torn up over money and legal issues.

Imagine your spouse being dragged into court because he or she missed a deadline in disposing of your estate.

To save some money, maybe you made your spouse the executor of your estate. Or maybe you died intestate, without a valid will. And your spouse feels either for personal protection or out of some sense of responsibility the need to be the executor.

What could be better than leaving your spouse in charge if you should die? Doesn't he or she know your wishes best?

A lot can be wrong with it.

He or she may be in shock after your death. Probably will be. Your spouse faces months of readjustment coping with your loss.

Put in charge of your estate, your spouse won't have a chance to grieve—and grief is necessary. Instead, he or she will be caught in a maelstrom of legal requirements, accounting, managing, and fighting. Yes, fighting.

A sister may wonder why you left her out. A grown child may say you promised to cancel the loan in the event of your death.

Money makes people do strange things. It's the reason many marriages break up. It's behind divisive family fights after the death or deaths of parents.

Planning your budget with your family—giving them a say in it, not just giving them orders—and having your estate plan worked out are ways to avoid those problems.

It also can save you from having the estate you leave behind eaten away by state and federal estate taxes and high administration fees.

Federal estate taxes kick in on anything above $600,000. What happens is that the government applies a tax of $192,000 upon the first $600,000 of the estate and then gives you a $192,000 credit. The tax rate is 32 percent on the first $600,000 of an estate. And it keeps going up incrementally after that. Thus, what's left to beneficiaries, other than your spouse, goes down in value rapidly after the credit is lost. With state taxes and administration fees, a $2 million estate can become worth only about $1.3 million to your heirs very quickly if you don't plan your estate wisely.

If $2 million sounds like a lot now, it won't when you get your investments going and your house paid off. You have to remember that inflation will push up the value of your assets and your holdings, but Congress must raise the $600,000 limit if it is to reflect those inflationary gains.

WHAT DO YOU NEED TO DO?

By filling out the information for your retirement plan, you have almost all the information you'll need to set up an estate plan. The one thing you don't have is the expertise of an estate planner and a lawyer.

And that's what you'll need.

Sure, there are books that will tell you how to draw up a will. And in half the states, handwritten wills are acceptable. But different states have different requirements covering who will serve as executor of your estate. Your particular circumstances need to be taken into account.

It would take a book to give you all the information you need to write your own will. It would take another book to tell you how to plan your estate. And it would take a bulletin service to keep you acquainted with all the changes in state and federal laws governing estates.

You don't need that. You need to hire an expert in your state on estate planning and to draw up a will.

That doesn't mean you can hand all the decisions to the estate planner and your lawyer, though. You have to make some tough choices. Evaluating your assets is one thing; knowing what to do with them in case of your death means evaluating even more precious things—your family and your friends.

In drawing up a will, you need to decide who will get your estate. Will your spouse need help? Will your children, even if they're grown, handle what you leave them wisely? If you have stepchildren, do you want them to get a share? Nieces? Nephews? Special friends? If your spouse remarries, do you want him or her to have full control over your bequest? What happens if you and your spouse die together? Who do you want to be executor? (Even estate lawyers have had problems handling estate matters when it was their spouse who died.) What about debts your heirs owe you? With young children, who do you want to care for them? What about mortgages you still owe? They unlike other debts can be passed along with the property to a beneficiary. Do you want to do that?

Make a list of beneficiaries and what you want to leave. Also draw up a list of any worries or concerns you have about how beneficiaries will handle your bequest.

This might lead you to set up trust accounts. There are numerous kinds. Following are the most common.

Living Trusts. These go into effect while you are still alive. In one form, it can be used to designate who will receive the property in the trust while you continue to receive income from the trust. You must give up control of the assets, though, to a trustee, who should be bonded to protect against mismanagement of the trust. The advantages are that you can bypass federal and state estate taxes, protect your assets if you become too ill or incompetent to manage your affairs, avoid probate and protect the privacy of your assets and, by having set the terms in the trust, distribute assets according to what you consider the best advantage for your beneficiaries.

Testamentary Trusts. These are trusts set up in your will. This is especially good for taking care of the needs of a young child who otherwise might not be able to handle the money. Mentally retarded or disabled children will need care even into adulthood. This kind of trust, while it can't avoid estate taxes, can take care of that need.

Bypass Trusts. These trusts allow you to pass on more money to your children without paying federal and state estate taxes. In your will, you simply designate a portion of the estate to go into a trust account for your youngsters, with your spouse as the beneficiary of the interest and income from the trust until his or her death. When that happens, the trust is dissolved, with the proceeds going to your kids but not being counted in your spouse's estate. That reduces the tax bite. It also gives your kids a chance to grow up. An off-shot of this is a voluntary by-pass trust that lets the surviving spouse decide whether or not the trust is needed at the time of your death.

Life Insurance Trusts. These take the proceeds from your life insurance policy and put them into a trust from which your surviving spouse can draw income, but the proceeds of which go directly to the children in the event of his or her death. This again reduces the estate value of the surviving spouse and lowers the tax bite on the estate.

There are other means of handling your estate. But these are good things to discuss with your estate planner.

Eventually, when you reach retirement and find out how much money you need to live on, you and your spouse might like to reduce your estate in another way if your assets are growing faster than you need.

You can gift up to $10,000 a person per year without any taxes. The only hitch is if you die suddenly other than in an accident or from some unexpected illness. Then the government might look at those gifts and decide you were trying to avoid estate taxes by giving the gifts in contemplation of death. Then those gifts could be subject to estate taxes.

In the meantime, though, go to a good lawyer and get a decent will made up. Tie up the loose ends of life now, so you don't have to worry about them. Just as by following the prescriptions in this book, I hope you won't find yourself worrying about your retirement but doing something to make it worthwhile.

Life is short. Time is short. But the best can be yet to come. Don't worry. Do something. Then you can be happier.

Glossary

Actuarial Table: A table broken down by age of the years people can be expected to live, given their race, sex, smoking habits, geographical area, occupations, and whether they eat pizza with double cheese or with anchovies. Used by insurance companies to justify the premiums they charge you for insurance. Not as useful as kitchen tables but more expensive, even if you hold the anchovies.

Adjusted Gross Income: Income minus the deductions allowed you for tax purposes. What you really have to live on.

Administration Fee: A charge usually associated with a mutual fund or limited partnership paid to those managing the fund or partnership for their services. These fees make you appreciate efficient managers.

AMEX: American Stock Exchange, as opposed to NYNEX, New York Stock Exchange. AMEX is for small- to medium-sized companies. The S for "stock" is deleted even for sexy issues.

Amortization: Payment of a debt, such as a mortgage, in installments or over time. Also a process by which people who develop payment debt formulas begin to look like Mortimer Sneerd.

Annual Policy: An insurance policy written for one year or renewed each year. For people who like to take life one year at a time.

Annuity: A contract that provides you an income, usually for life or a specified number of years. Often offered by insurance companies, but only if you give them a big chunk of dough to start with. You knew it, didn't you?

Appreciation: The increase in value, either in price or number, of an asset. Something you appreciate.

Asset: Any item that has value, including a loving spouse. But for economic purposes, it's anything you can buy or sell. For retirement purposes, think stocks, bonds, mutual funds, rental, or other real estate and, even, whole-life insurance and annuities.

Back-End Load: Shame on you. See Load.

Balance Sheet: A financial form divided into assets, liabilities, and net worth, or owner's equity. Also called a net worth statement, although a negative net worth unbalances people.

Balloon Loan: A loan that requires the borrower to make a series of small payments and then a big final payment. If you can make the final payment, you throw a party complete with balloons.

Basis: The purchase price of an asset for tax purposes. It can be what you paid for it, what somebody else paid for it, if they give it to you, or the price or its value at the time you inherit it. You determine your gain or loss by subtracting the basis, so you can never sell without basis.

Bear Market: A market in which stocks or bonds or real estate decline in value. A time when many investors in those markets hibernate.

Beneficiary: A person named to receive property or other consideration, as in a will or life insurance policy. Say thank you.

Bequest: What a beneficiary gets from a will. It is not considered polite to request a bequest.

Bill of Sale: Proof in written form that ownership of a piece of property has been transferred from a seller to a buyer. That's helpful if you've ever been sold a bill of goods.

Bills: Debt securities issued by the U.S. Treasury for terms of less than one year. That's B and it rhymes with T and it stands for T-bills. T-bills are sold to cover the nation's big debt. And that's D and it rhymes with T and that means Trouble.

Blue-chip Stock: Shares of a company with a long track record of profit, dividend payments, and appreciation. Even in a bear market, it's wise not to cash in all of your blue chips.

Bond: A written promise to pay a fixed sum of money at a future date and at a specific interest rate. Used by governments to finance deficits (U.S. Savings Bonds), by municipalities to finance civic improvements, and by private corporations to buy equipment and build factories and offices. Also, Ward Bond: Actor noted for role on *Wagon Train* and for phrases such as "Jumpin' jehosafat" and "gul durn," which are more associated with speculative stocks than with bonds.

Book Value: The total assets of a business, minus its liabilities, divided by the number of outstanding shares. If book value exceeds the market price of the stock, you can make book that the business may be looked at by a takeover specialist.

Broker: An intermediary or representative who acts as an agent in the buying or selling of investments. A person interested in getting you to buy and sell as often as possible as long as it doesn't leave you so broke you can't afford another transaction.

Bull Market: When the bear market investors come out of hibernation and run wild, like a bunch of bulls. Stock rises when bulls go crazy.

Call: An option to buy stock at a specified price at specified times. The caller pays the seller a fee for the option and can't reverse the charges, even if the call (the option price) doesn't get through.

Capital Gains or Losses: The difference between the basis for an asset and what it is sold for, after taking into account the costs of holding the asset. There's nothing funny about capital gains and losses.

Cash Value: The cash fund accumulated in a whole- or universal- or total-life insurance policy. Cash value is the savings feature of these policies. And the small savings features of such policies are one reason people sold on term insurance prefer a cashless society.

Causa Mortis: Latin meaning "on account of death." If a person gives a gift to you causa mortis, it means he expects to die and you should expect to pay taxes on the gift.

Caveat Emptor: Latin meaning "let the buyer beware." A good thing to keep in mind whenever somebody offers you a deal too good to believe.

Certificate of Deposit: A bond issued by a bank maturing in from 30 days to 5 years. Often called CDs, they are an easy way to get started into investing. And an easy way to save so you can buy a CD player.

Churning: A broker making you broke by trading in your account to generate more commission income for himself or herself. Another good reason to keep in mind "caveat emptor." It makes investors' stomachs churn.

Collateral: Property or money pledged as security for the repayment of a loan. In the case of bonds, it means the bond will be secured by the equipment it buys or factory it builds. In the case of a mortgage, it's the house or building the mortgage buys. When between two people, it is bilateral collateral.

Commercial Paper: Short-term debt issued by big business.

Commodity: The material an enterprise needs rather than the enterprise itself, everything from hog bellies, to orange juice, to gold, silver, and other precious metals. When you go to the grocery, you bring home a lot of commodities.

Common Stock: The stock that gives you an ownership interest in an enterprise, complete with voting rights, rather than a stake in a company's debt (which is a bond). Preferred stock also gives you a stake in the company, a preferred position in getting dividends, and a pay-out before common shareholders in the case a business is liquidated. Common stock prices tend to rise faster than preferred shares, though, offering a greater chance at capital gains (or losses). Getting rich with preferred stock is uncommon; less so with common stock.

Compound Interest: Interest earned is added to an account, and the rate of interest is then applied to the new total in the account. The compounding occurs over a set period, which can be daily for some savings accounts at banks trying to hold your interest.

Conservator: Person appointed to take care of someone's financial affairs, usually because of disability.

Convertible Bonds: Bonds that can be converted into shares of common stock. Sort of flip-flop securities.

Coupon Rate: Stated rate of return on a fixed-income investment. You go to a bank when you clip these coupons, rather than the grocery.

Current Asset: An asset that can be quickly converted to cash so you can stay current with your bills.

Current Liability: Debts that are due for payment in the near future, usually less than a year. For example, your mortgage has monthly current liabilities, though you aren't obligated to repay the full amount of the loan for several years. Taxes are current liabilities. Also known as bills, except in investment circles.

Current Ratio: The ratio of current assets to current liabilities. If a company has less than $1 in current assets for each $1 in current liabilities that it must pay (for example, 0.9:1), it doesn't have enough money to pay its bills. A ratio of 2:1 ($2 in current assets to $1 in current liabilities) is preferred.

Current Value: The price you could get on the market for an asset.

Debentures: A kind of collateral bond that's secured only by a company's general assets rather than by any specific asset.

Debt-to-Equity Ratio: Ratio of total debt to equity, with equity being assets minus liabilities.

Depreciation: Not exactly the opposite of appreciation. Depreciation is the allocation of the cost of an asset, such as plant or equipment, over its useful life. It is then deducted from the income that a business venture earns, reducing taxes on that income. Businesses appreciate that.

Discount Rate: Interest rate charged by the Federal Reserve System on loans to banks that are part of the system. Unfortunately, we can't discount it.

Diversification: A means for investors to reduce their overall risk by investing in a variety of different types of investments, proving the good of the advice that there is security in numbers.

Dividends: Payments by companies to their stockholders. The ends are profits and stockholders divide them.

Dollar-Cost Averaging: Buying stocks or similar investments in incremental periods with a set amount of money. This averages out the price fluctuations of stocks so that your investment in the company will reflect the company's general trend of growth, recognizing that sometimes the price of stocks fluctuates due to forces unrelated to the company's performance.

Dow Jones Industrial Average: A mix of 500 stocks used to gauge the overall performance of the stock market for traders. Also called the "Dow," which in a bear market sometimes looks like a cow.

Earnings Per Common Share: The earnings of a company, its profits, after taking out taxes and the dividends paid to preferred stockholders and then divided by the outstanding shares of common stock. Comparing earnings per share of different companies is a means for common shareholders or potential shareholders to evaluate the companies' performance.

Equity: Assets minus liabilities. Same as net worth. It's fairest when it's highest.

ERISA: The Employee Retirement Income Security Act, which set up protection for pensions.

Estate: Everything a person owns.

Executor: Person appointed to carry out the terms of a will.

Exemption: Release from an obligation to pay certain taxes.

Fiduciary: Person or institution that has been placed in a position of trust to act for the benefit of another person and has a legal duty to do so.

FIFO: First In, First Out. An accounting method to value inventory for tax purposes. In the case of the sale of shares of stock, the government assumes that the first stock shares you bought are the first ones you'll sell unless you can prove otherwise.

401(K) Plan: A pension plan arrangement in which a person is allowed to deduct from his income up to $7,800 and place it into a personal retirement account over which he or she has investment control. Money in the account grows tax deferred, and usually employers will match 50 cents for each dollar an employee contributes to the account. There is a 10 percent tax penalty for the withdrawal of any money from the account prior to age 59½.

Front-End Load: See Load.

General Partner: In a limited partnership, the person or group of people who put together the investment proposal and then sold shares to investors.

Ginny Mae: Government national mortgage association, which sells securities (often called Ginny Maes) backed by its mortgages on selected types of home mortgages.

GNMA: See Ginny Mae.

Growth Stock: Shares of a company that seeks rapid growth, usually at the expense of paying dividends. Such a company is usually young, will have higher than normal debt to equity ratios, and thus is riskier than older enterprises but also provides greater rewards.

Guardian: Person given legal custody of another person who is legally considered unable to care for himself or herself.

Health Insurance: There are two types: One covers the loss of income due to disability, the other pays for the health care costs of someone who is ill.

Holographic Statement: A financial statement by a firm showing how its income was spent and how much remains after expenses. One hopes income is more than outgo.

Income Stock: Stock with substantial dividends but with little capital growth.

Index Fund: A mutual fund that has a highly diversified portfolio of stock, usually in the same basket as one of the various stock market indexes.

Individual Retirement Account: A personal retirement account in which people can put up to $2,000 in income each year to grow tax deferred until retirement. For individuals with less than $25,000 in adjusted gross income, the contribution is fully deductible; for couples, a $2,200 contribution is fully deductible at up to $40,000 in adjusted gross income.

Inflation: Increase in prices. That rate of inflation is determined by the Consumer Price Index, which is made up of a basket of goods that is weighted in accord to how an average of the population purchases them, which is why they always seem to rise faster for you.

Insolvency: Lacking the cash to pay one's financial obligations, illiquid while awash in bills.

Insured: Person on whom an insurance policy is taken out.

Interest: Money paid by a borrower in addition to the amount borrowed. The rate of interest is that additional amount over the amount borrowed and then calculated as an annual percentage.

Intestate: Dying without a will. It leaves the heirs in a state of limbo.

Keogh: A pension plan for the self-employed that allows tax deductible contributions of up to $30,000 a year into accounts on which the tax is deferred until retirement and on which they then may pay reduced taxes.

Legacy: Something you leave to somebody in a will, not including real estate.

Leverage: Borrowing money to make money. Essentially, a person uses borrowed funds or other debt instruments to try to increase the return on an investment by not tying up too much of his or her own money. It's a high-risk game, even though banks finance a lot of the leveraged buyouts of corporations now in vogue.

Liability: A debt for which there is a legal obligation to repay.

Lien: A legal claim against a piece of property meant to make sure a debt is repaid. Popular song: Don't lien on me.

LIFO: Last in, first out. Another accounting method for valuing inventories, but one the IRS doesn't appreciate.

Limit Order: An order to buy or sell at a specified price.

Liquidate: To pay a debt.

Liquidity: The ability to pay debts, which means having cash or other securities easily convertible to cash to pay off your debts. Another way to think of liquidity is to be awash in cash.

Limited Partnership: A partnership formed for a limited period of time, usually five to seven years, which invests in a particular type of asset, such as apartment buildings, office buildings, equipment, and the like. Partners share in the profits of the enterprise, as well as certain deductions, until the partnership is dissolved, at which time the investor gets his money back. If it's still there. The limited partners' losses are limited to their investments, which often start at $100,000 each. Some limit.

Load: Sales charges to a buyer of mutual funds, sometimes taken up front (front-end loads) or on leaving (back-end loads or redemption fees). Low loads are up-front sales charges that are simply less than the regular 8.5 percent load many funds usually charge. Loads reduce return by reducing the amount actually invested. They are heavy and a bother.

Long-term Assets: Assets, such as plant and equipment, which are not easily converted to cash.

Long-term Liabilities: A mortgage on the plant or building, a 30-year bond. Liabilities for which payments are due more than a year away. Out of sight, but never out of mind.

Margin: Investing in stocks using borrowed money to help finance the investment. The risk is that if there is a margin call, the investor may have to dig into his own savings to pay it if sale of the stock won't cover the debt. In 1929 when some people put only 10 percent of their money down on stocks, margin calls led some to go over the edge—of the Empire State Building.

Marginal Tax Bracket: The tax rate a person pays on the next dollar they earn.

Market Index: A basket of stocks, the price fluctuations of which are calculated to give a picture of the direction the overall market is moving.

Market Order: An order to buy or sell at the current market price. But because a free market is never orderly, some investors place limit orders too.

Market Risk: The chance that an overall change in the market will affect stocks despite their individual record and performance. In a free market, that happens.

Market Value: The price an investor can get for a stock, a house, a piece of property at a particular point in time. It's the only real value any investment has, no matter what was paid for it.

Maturity: Date at which a loan or bond becomes due for repayment of the principal that was borrowed. And hopefully the debtor will be mature enough to pay the debt.

Money Market: The market for short-term securities, such as certificates of deposit, T-bills, some corporate notes, and other things that pass for money.

Money Market Fund: A mutual fund invested in money market securities, hopefully increasing your money.

Mortgage: A loan made to purchase a piece of property, of two main types: fixed rate, in which the interest rate is fixed for the term of the loan, and variable rate, in which the interest rate and repayment schedule can change every year to three years. The rates on variable rate mortgages are often tied to the rate on T-bills and other government securities, moving up or down with them within certain limits.

Mortgage Bonds: Debt securities with mortgages as collateral.

Municipal Bonds: Tax-exempt bonds issued by state and local governments.

Municipal Funds: Mutual funds invested in tax-exempt municipal bonds. Sometimes called munies, which confuses Paul Muni's heirs.

Mutual Funds: Investment companies that pool investors' money to invest in securities. These companies are open-ended in that they will issue new shares when investors want to invest and will redeem those shares when an investor wants to sell. Investors buy directly from the company, with the value of shares determined by the market prices of the securities of the fund.

Mutual Insurance Company: Insurance companies owned directly by policyholders rather than stockholders.

Net Asset Value: The value per share of a mutual fund's portfolio of assets.

Net Income: Income after expenses, including deductions for depreciation and taxes.

Net Worth: Assets minus liabilities (equity). The bigger the fish, the more the net worth.

Nonmarket Risk: The risk of investing in an individual firm not related to general market risk. Also known as life is not fair.

Notary: A public officer who takes oaths and witnesses signatures on documents. They "seal" the bargains.

Notes: Securities that mature in one to five years. Can you hit the high notes is the question.

NYSE: New York Stock Exchange. Place where they keep "The Big Board."

Odd Lot: Stock is normally traded in lots of 100. When it isn't, it is odd, and they make you pay more to trade it.

Option: An exclusive right to buy or sell securities or real estate at a specified price at a specified time. To get the right you have to buy the option.

Option Price: The price at which the holder of an option or warrant may purchase the securities or property. You have no option but to sell.

Ordinary Life Insurance: Whole-life or term life insurance. Nothing extraordinary.

Over-the-Counter: A market for stocks and bonds not listed on security exchanges in which dealers sell shares directly to clients. As with headache medicine, some people prefer buying off the shelf instead.

Partnership: An agreement between two or more people to run a business and share its profits and losses.

Par Value: For common stock, a price usually set well below the initial offering price for a stock. Most stock trades well above par, so the term has little meaning except that if a company's net worth falls below the total par value of all its stock, it can't pay dividends. For preferred stock, it is the basis for preferred dividends that a company is obligated to pay before paying any dividends to common shareholders. For bonds, it is the price a company must pay to redeem the bond. That's par for the course.

Pension: A benefit paid to a former employee upon retirement or to that former employee's dependents if he or she is dead.

Personal Property: Usually anything that can be owned other than real estate. For retirement planning purposes, it's anything that isn't an investment or real estate. It's nobody's business.

Points: A charge by the lender for making a loan. The points are percentage points and are a one-time payment on the amount of the loan usually having to be paid at the time a sale is concluded. For example, when you take out a $100,000 loan to buy a house, the lender may charge you 2 or 3 points, worth $2,000 or $3,000. You may negotiate with the seller of the house to pick up some of the points in exchange, perhaps, for a slightly higher price. Why you should always ask, "What's the points?"

Policy Loan: The amount borrowed against a life insurance policy's cash value.

Portfolio: An investor's investments. They can be divided into groups, such as a stock portfolio or bond portfolio. But an investor's portfolio includes all the financial assets he or she holds.

Portfolio Insurance: A strategy in which investors sell options or futures against the underlying stock in a portfolio to offset price declines. Investors were burned by this insurance in the 1987 crash.

Power of Attorney: The authority to act as the agent for another person, for specific business matters or in general.

Preferred Stock: See Common Stock.

Premium: For a warrant, the market price less the exercise value, which is the option price less the market price for a stock. For a convertible bond, the market price less its conversion value or the debt value of a bond. For instance, the amount of money charged by an insurance company to a policy holder.

Present Value: The value in today's dollars of future income. It's figured by reducing the value of that future income by an interest rate meant to reflect inflation. A guesstimate.

Price-to-Earnings Ratio: The market price of a stock divided by its earnings per share. The ratio is used to determine whether a stock is reasonably priced. Historically, a ratio of 13:1 is considered reasonable. At the time of the 1987 stock market crash, the ratio for the whole market was 19:1. The crash took it to 13:1. Got it?

Principal: For the borrower, the amount of the debt not including interest charges. Also, the person primarily responsible for the debt. For the lender or investor, the actual money invested by a person. In case of debt, you want to eat away the principal. In the case of savings, you don't.

Probate: Court procedure that determines the validity of a will. Sometimes called living death.

Profit: What's left after you pay all the expenses. Then the government comes along and adds additional expenses called taxes.

Prospectus: A required document to be provided by those issuing new securities for sale to the public. It gives the financial position of the company making the offering, the use of the money raised by the offering, any sales or redemption charges in the case of mutual funds, minimum investments required, and a host of other information so prospective investors can evaluate the offering.

Put: An option to sell stock at a specific price over a specified time. Once the stock is sold, the option is shot. See Option.

Rate of Return: The dividends and the increases in the market price of a stock or bond or other investment divided by its purchase price.

Real Return: The rate of return reduced by the inflation rate.

Rebate: A return to the buyer of a part of his payment.

Recession: Unofficially, when your neighbor is unemployed. When you are, it's a depression. Officially, two successive quarters in which the Gross National Product has declined after reducing its growth for inflation. A recession is bad economic news when it happens; it is good news in contemplation if there is high inflation.

Residuary Estate: In a will, it's the property that isn't specifically given to any person. Usually, at reading of the will, the executor will say, ". . . and all the rest of my property I leave to my beloved . . ." and everybody holds their breath.

Return: In taxes, a statement showing the federal government what you think you owe it or should get back from it after attempting to fill it out, usually erroneously. In investments, the profit from your investment before filling out your taxes where you try to make it look smaller than it really is.

REIT: Real Estate Investment Trust. A form of mutual fund that invests in properties. Some invest in rental properties, such as offices or apartments. Some invest in mortgages. They are a simple way to invest in real estate without the hassle of actually owning property.

Retained Earnings: The profit or earnings a company retains rather than pay them out as dividends. Finders keepers.

Rollover: Either a switch from one kind of investment to another, or a restructuring of a pension account in which the government gives you 60 days to take the proceeds and put them into a new account before charging you a 10 percent penalty tax on the proceeds. Hopefully, you roll over into clover.

Round Lot: The basic unit in which stocks are traded, usually at 100 units.

S&P: Standard & Poor's, a firm that computes market indexes and rates bonds.

SEC: Securities and Exchange Commission. It regulates the securities industry. If you have a complaint, call them.

Second Market: See Over-the-Counter.

Securities: Stocks, bonds, and other financial instruments of corporations and governments that are sold to raise money for the business and bought to make money by investors.

Securities and Exchange Commission: See SEC.

Selling Short: A speculative technique in which a person borrows some securities and sells them expecting their price to decline. If they do, he buys them back and returns them to the lender while making a profit for himself. If they don't, he's caught short.

Simple Interest: Interest paid only on the principal without adding in previous interest paid to the principal.

Speculation: Another word for investing, differing only in degree. To speculate, you are hoping for a big return from a venture in which there is high risk you may lose your money. To invest, you are hoping for a return that beats inflation in which you hope you won't lose your money. To people seeking your money, anything you give them is always an investment not a speculation.

Standard & Poor's: See S&P.

Stock Split: When a company increases the number of shares of its stock to lower its price, giving stockholders the new shares.

Stop-Limit Order: An order to buy or sell securities at the market price when a certain price is reached.

Stop-Loss Order: An order to buy or sell securities at the market price when a certain price is reached.

Striking Price: The price paid by the holder of an option to use that option.

Tax Credit: A reduction in taxes, usually by a specific dollar amount or as a percentage of earnings or losses.

Tax Deferred: You earn now and pay Uncle Sam later. Interest earned in IRAs is tax deferred. While the account builds, you don't pay income taxes on the earnings. But when you withdraw money, the gains in the account are taxed.

Tax Exempt (or Tax Free): You earn now and keep later. Also known as tax free. Earnings from municipal bonds or municipal bond mutual funds aren't taxed by the federal government.

Tax Free: See Tax Exempt.

Tax Shelter: A venture in which its owners or investors put money with the promise that either a part or all of their earnings will be tax free or tax deferred.

Term Insurance: Any insurance, life or auto or casualty, that provides coverage only over a specified period.

Treasury Bill: See Bills.

Treasury Stocks: Stock shares in a company held by the company or by the issuer of the stock.

True Yield: The return on an investment reduced by taxes and expenses and then divided by its market or purchase price which is then expressed as a percentage. This is the only true measure of what you get, rather than the broker, the administrator, and Uncle Sam.

Trust: A legal arrangement by which one person takes care of another's investments or property for the benefit of another. Also part of the name of Johnny Carson's first major TV show: "Who Do You Trust?"

Underwriter: In insurance, an insurance company employee who selects business for the company that will result in an average risk of loss no greater than that for all that particular class of business. In investment, a dealer that agrees to buy all or part of a new stock or bond issue from a company with the intention of selling it to the public later.

Universal Life Insurance: A type of whole-life policy in which the policyholder can vary within certain limits the amount of payments, the time when they are paid, and the death benefit.

Variable Annuities: A type of annuity, usually sold by insurance companies, that is invested like a mutual fund and provides returns that vary by the investment experience of the fund in which it is invested. You don't get the guarantees of a regular annuity, but you also don't risk tying up large sums of money at low rates.

Variable Life Insurance: A life insurance policy that has a guaranteed minimum death benefit and also increases in cash value. The cash value is invested and, depending on the choice of investments, can either grow rapidly or become nonexistent, much like any other investment.

Warrants: Guarantees that let you purchase a company's stock at specified prices within certain time limits.

Whole-Life Insurance: A type of life insurance with a savings feature as well as a death benefit. It can put a hole in your pocket. See Cash Value.

Will: A document in which you decide who gets what in case you die. You will, so you need one.

Yield: The return on an investment divided by its market price and expressed as a percentage. Yield means literally to give up. It's what your investments give up to you, and to managers, administrators, and Uncle Sam. After paying them, you sometimes feel like giving up. Don't.

Index